Fun Independent Practice Pages

Geometry and Measurement

by
Bob Olenych

SCHOLASTIC
PROFESSIONAL BOOKS

New York • Toronto • London • Auckland • Sydney
Mexico City • New Delhi • Hong Kong • Buenos Aires

DEDICATION

To all of my students who had geometry come alive for them through
line design creations.

Cover design by Josué Castilleja
Cover illustration by Mike Moran
Interior design by Melinda Belter
Interior illustrations by Steve Cox, Jared Lee, and Anne Kennedy

ISBN 0-439-38526-1

1 2 3 4 5 6 7 8 9 10   40   10 09 08 07 06 05 04 03

Table of Contents

Introduction

GEOMETRY AND MEASUREMENT ARE FUN CONCEPTS

Geometry and measurement are concepts that I have always looked forward to teaching. By incorporating line designs into my teaching, I have been successful at making geometry come alive for my students. By showing students how to make some very simple line designs, I incorporate the vocabulary that they need to use (such as right, acute, or obtuse angles; rays; and congruent) when we discuss designs, and they are also taught how to use a protractor to construct angles of various sizes. Once they have had an opportunity to create some line designs such as the ones in this book, I generally encourage students to create their own line designs. How to use a compass and how to accurately divide a page into halves and quarters is demonstrated to them. Over the years, my students have created portfolios of breathtaking designs that have been displayed and shared with the class. Students who have been adept at using the compass or protractor, or those who have created an interesting design, will often act as mentors to help others achieve success. I strongly encourage you to try this approach with your class and I'm confident that you will notice that your class really gets hooked on geometry.

WHAT YOU'LL FIND IN THIS BOOK

This book offers a collection of geometry and measurement activities for a broad range of skills and abilities. The book begins with activities involving geometry, then progresses to measurement. The puzzles are arranged according to skill, from easy to difficult, and conclude with word problems that focus on liquid, weight, and time measurement. You can match the needs of your students and target a specific skill by checking the skill description listed in the table of contents.

I've also included a student reference page that provides a list of measures that students will find useful. This page will prove to be especially helpful when students are doing various measurement activities that may require them to convert an answer, such as feet to miles or gallons to quarts.

Name _____ Student Reference Page
Date _____

Table of Measures

TIME

60 seconds = 1 minute	365 days = 1 year
60 minute = 1 hour	366 days = 1 leap year
24 hours = 1 day	12 months = 1 year
7 days = 1 week	10 years = 1 decade
52 weeks = 1 year	100 years = 1 century
1,000 years = 1 millennium	

LENGTH

Standard	Metric
12 inches = 1 foot	10 millimeters = 1 centimeter
3 feet = 1 yard	10 centimeters = 1 decimeter
1,760 yards = 1 mile	10 decimeters = 1 meter
5,280 feet = 1 mile	100 centimeters = 1 meter
1,000 meters = 1 kilometer	

WEIGHT

Standard	Metric
16 ounces = 1 pound	1,000 grams = 1 kilogram
2,000 pounds = 1 ton	1,000 kilograms = 1 metric ton

LIQUID

Standard	Metric
8 fluid ounces = 1 cup	1,000 milliliters = 1 liter
2 cups = 1 pint	1,000 liters = 1 kiloliter
4 cups = 1 quart	
2 pints = 1 quart	
4 quarts = 1 gallon	

SCHOLASTIC PROFESSIONAL BOOKS   FUN INDEPENDENT PRACTICE PAGES: GEOMETRY AND MEASUREMENT   **45**

HOW TO USE THIS BOOK

Be sure to use these puzzles in a way that best suits the needs of your class. You may find it helpful to assign certain puzzles as practice work to follow a lesson, as review work, or as homework. You also may want to have students work on different puzzles depending on the skills each student needs to practice. The beauty of these activities is that almost all of them are self-correcting. Whether they are solving a riddle or breaking a code, students are encouraged to check each problem so they can finish the puzzle successfully.

CONNECTIONS TO THE MATH STANDARDS

Most of the puzzles in this book target NCTM 2000 objectives listed under the Geometry and Measurement Standards. These objectives include measuring with customary and metric systems, calculating area, perimeter, and volume, as well as constructing and measuring angles, and using geometry terminology. This book is packed with exercises that require students to use measurement and geometry in a variety of formats, including word problems and multiple-step equations.

I am confident that your students, like mine, will enjoy this collection of puzzles and reap the benefits of practicing these essential skills.

Bob Olenych

Name _____ Date _____

Did You Hear?

Unscramble each of the geometry terms found along the left side of the page.
Print the correct word so that each letter occupies a box to the right of the scrambled
word. By reading down in the shaded boxes, you will reveal the answer to the
following riddle.

Hint: Numbers 4 and 9
name tools you use for
geometry work!

Did you hear about King Kong
sitting on top of the Empire State Building?

1. IDESS

2. GHRIT

3. CLECIREMIS

4. TORTRACROP

5. TEXREV

6. ENTCONGUR

7. GLETRINA

8. YRSA

9. APOCSMS

10. TEACU

11. CELRIC

12. BUSMOHR

13. USTEBO

14. GELNA

15. DREEEG

,

Never mind . . . __ __ __ __ __   __ __ __ __ __ __ __ __ __ __ .

Geometry Terminology (geometry terms: definitions)

Name _____   Date _____

Let's Talk Geometry!

Complete the following statements by filling in each blank with the correct word from the answer boxes below. To answer some of these questions, refer to the diagram. Take the word that is found at the end of the statement and write it above the answer in the code box. When you have finished, you will decode the following riddle.

What's the safest way to talk to a guard dog?

1. An _____ is made up of two rays that share the same vertex.   **YOU**

2. A tool designed as a half circle, a _____ measures angles and has two scales.   **AWAY**

3. An _____ triangle has three sides of equal length.   **THAT**

4. The _____ of an angle is the point where two straight lines or line segments meet to form an angle.   **BE**

5. A _____ is a polygon with three sides.   **AS**

6. Angle ∠ NOY is an _____ angle, measuring less than 90°.   **CAN**

7. A _____ is an instrument used to draw a circle.   **MAKE**

8. None of the sides of a _____ triangle is equal in length to the others.   **AS**

9. Angle ∠ ZOY is a _____ angle that forms a square corner and measures 90°.   **ARE**

10. Angle ∠ MOZ is an _____ angle measuring between 90° and 180°.   **YOU**

11. Two sides of an _____ triangle are of equal length.   **FAR**

12. Angle ∠ MON is a _____ angle, measuring 180°.   **SURE**

COMPASS	STRAIGHT	EQUILATERAL	ANGLE	RIGHT	SCALENE

ISOSCELES	PROTRACTOR	TRIANGLE	OBTUSE	ACUTE	VERTEX

SCHOLASTIC PROFESSIONAL BOOKS   FUN INDEPENDENT PRACTICE PAGES: GEOMETRY AND MEASUREMENT   7

Name _____ Date _____

Match It #1

Match the geometric terms on the left side of the page to the correct shape on the right. Use a ruler or a straightedge to draw a line from the term to the shape (dot to dot). Your line will pass through a number and a letter. The number tells you where to write your letter in the code boxes to answer the riddle below.

What should you do if Godzilla suddenly starts to cry?

pentagon •

ray •   **8**   **L**

intersecting lines • **12**   **N**

rectangle • **3**

       M

line •   **6**   **E**

      A

triangle • **14** **N** **B**

point • **10** **2** **9**

       D

perpendicular lines •   ☐

circle • **4**   **U**

line segment • **13** **7** **A**

square •   **5** **F** **R**

hexagon • **11** **1** **L** **I**

parallel lines •

octagon •

1	2	3	4		5	6		7	8	9	10	11	12	13	14

FUN INDEPENDENT PRACTICE PAGES: GEOMETRY AND MEASUREMENT

SCHOLASTIC PROFESSIONAL BOOKS

Name _____ Date _____

Look Out Below

Find pairs of congruent figures by matching a shape with a letter to a congruent shape with a number. The number indicates where the letter should go in the code box below. Complete the activity to solve the following riddle.

Why did the little girl pour water over the balcony?

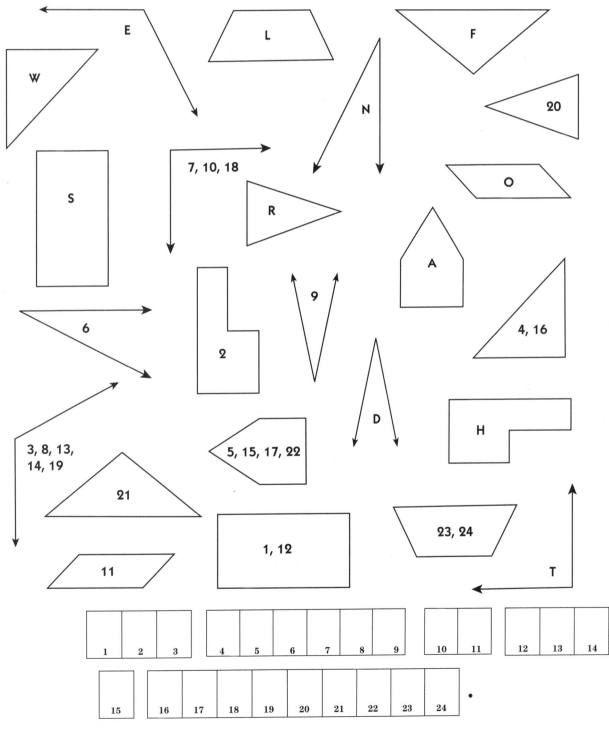

Name _____ Date _____

Campfires Made Easy

Hint: Trace the first shape and cut it out.

The four shapes in each row are congruent. The message to the left of first shape tells you what to find. Study the three shapes to the right of the first shape. Identify which one is as a result of a slide, turn, or flip of the first shape. For each "find a flip" problem, a line shows if the flip is horizontal or vertical. When you locate the correct shape, the number in the shape tells you where to write the word in the code boxes below.

How can a camper make a fire with just one stick?

FIND A FLIP.	4 WAS	5 ARE	7 IS
FIND A SLIDE.	5 WHETHER	3 IF	7 POSSIBLY
FIND A ¼ TURN.	8 A	6 THE	2 AM
FIND A SLIDE.	8 AN	4 THE	9 A
FIND A FLIP.	1 IT'S	5 ITS	6 THIS
FIND A ¼ TURN.	8 THREE	5 ONE	2 TWO
FIND A SLIDE.	6 SOFT	4 HARD	2 EASY
FIND A ¼ TURN.	6 STICK	1 TWIG	3 BRANCH
FIND A FLIP.	9 MATCH	7 CANDLE	4 LANTERN

1	2	3	4	5	6	7	8	9	.

Name _____ Date _____

Psst ... Let Me Tell You

Look at each row carefully and determine which figure in each row is not congruent to the other figures. When you find the incongruent shape, the number in the shape tells you where to write the word in the code boxes below in order to decode the riddle.

Why didn't the fisherman believe what the bluefin tuna was saying?

5 WORM	1 BOY	4 HORSE	2 TAIL	3 STORY
2 A	5 THESE	1 THE	4 THOSE	6 AN
2 ALSO	4 TO	3 TWO	5 TOO	1 SOME
4 BIRD'S	6 CAT'S	5 SHEEP'S	3 COW'S	2 TUNA'S
5 LOOKED	1 APPEARED	2 WALKED	4 SOUNDED	3 BURPED
2 SLEEPY	5 SCRATCHY	6 FISHY	4 FUNNY	1 SMOKEY

1	2	3	4	5	6

Name _____   Date _____

Why Do Fowls Lay Eggs?

In the chart below, determine the measure of the missing angle in the shaded box. When you have determined its size, find that answer in the code box below. Then write the word from the problem above the answer and reveal the solution to the riddle.

∠ X	∠ Y	∠ Z	ANGLE SUM
35°	35°	= EGGS	= 180°
= THEM	55°	90°	= 180°
78°	= BREAK	36°	= 180°
70°	95°	= AND	= 180°
63°	= BECAUSE	72°	= 180°
= IF	27°	112°	= 180°
90°	35°	= DROPPED	= 180°
28°	32°	= THEY	= 180°
= THEY'D	123°	27°	= 180°
64°	= DUCKS	49°	= 180°
= LAY	83°	48°	= 180°
31°	112°	= HENS	= 180°

67	15	37	49	110	45

30	66	41	120	55	35

Name _____ Date _____

Housebound

Determine the sizes of the unknown angles without using a protractor. Then find the answer in the code box below. Write the word from the problem above the answer and reveal the solution to the following riddle.

Why was the little mouse afraid to leave his home?

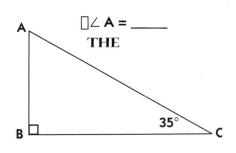

☐∠ A = _____
THE

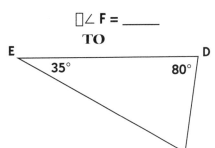

☐∠ F = _____
TO

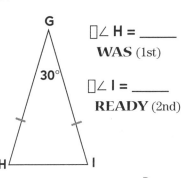

☐∠ H = _____
WAS (1st)

☐∠ I = _____
READY (2nd)

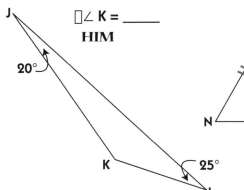

☐∠ K = _____
HIM

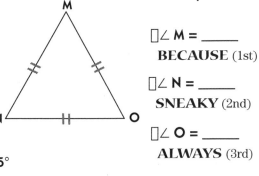

☐∠ M = _____
BECAUSE (1st)

☐∠ N = _____
SNEAKY (2nd)

☐∠ O = _____
ALWAYS (3rd)

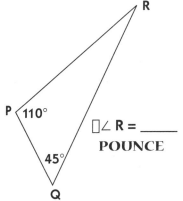

☐∠ R = _____
POUNCE

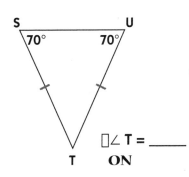

☐∠ T = _____
ON

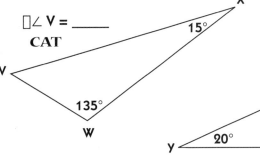

☐∠ V = _____
CAT

☐∠ Z = _____
HARRY

60°	20°	55°	60°	30°	75°

60°	75°	65°	25°	40°	135°

•

13

Name _____ Date _____

Fly on the Wall

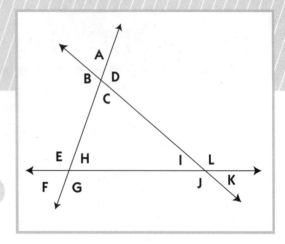

Solve the following problems WITHOUT USING A PROTRACTOR! Instead, use the measurements given in each problem and refer to the diagram at the right. When you have determined the size of the unknown angle, find that answer in the code box below. Then write the word from the problem above the answer to reveal the solution to the following riddle.

Hint:
Each problem gives a unique set of measurements for the angles.

Why do flies walk across the ceilings in a house?

1. If ∠ H = 70°, then ∠ F =   = **LIKELY**

2. If ∠ A = 60°, then ∠ D =   = **ON**

3. If ∠ C = 53°, then ∠ D =   = **THEY**

4. If ∠ J = 115°, then ∠ I =   = **ACROSS**

5. If ∠ E = 125°, then ∠ H =   = **FLOOR**

6. If ∠ I = 45°, then ∠ L =   = **THEM**

7. If ∠ E = 122°, then ∠ G =   = **SOMEONE**

8. If ∠ C = 70°, and ∠ H = 60°, then ∠ I =   = **THE**

9. If ∠ H = 49°, and ∠ I = 62°, then ∠ C =   = **WALKED**

10. If ∠ C = 31°, and ∠ H = 78°, then ∠ I =   = **HIGHLY**

11. If ∠ F = 50°, and ∠ K = 55°, then ∠ C =   = **STEP**

12. If ∠ D = 110°, and ∠ E = 110°, then ∠ I =   = **IF**

13. If ∠ B = 113°, and ∠ F = 47°, then ∠ I =   = **IT'S**

14. If ∠ K = 54°, and ∠ A = 66°, then ∠ H =   = **WOULD**

66	71	70	122	60	75	120

135	40	127	69	65	50	55

14

Name _____ Date _____

Why Are They Staring?

To decode this riddle your task is to construct angles using your protractor. These angles should be the size indicated (for example, ↖ **50°**). The line that you draw will go through a number. This number tells you where to write the word on the lines below.

Why were the kids staring hard at the orange juice container?

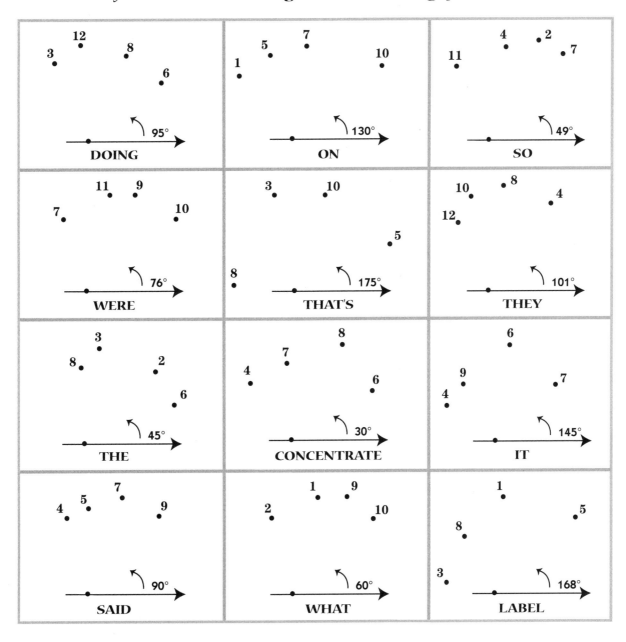

95° DOING	130° ON	49° SO
76° WERE	175° THAT'S	101° THEY
45° THE	30° CONCENTRATE	145° IT
90° SAID	60° WHAT	168° LABEL

```
___ ___ ___ ___   ___ ___
 1   2   3   4     5   6
                            .
___ ___ ___ ___   ___ ___
 7   8   9  10    11  12
```

FUN INDEPENDENT PRACTICE PAGES: GEOMETRY AND MEASUREMENT

Name _____ Date _____

Squirrel Talk

To decode this riddle, your task is to use your protractor to construct an angle at each end of a straight line. After constructing the two angles, measure the third angle and record its size in the space provided. Now find this answer in the code box below and write the word from the problem above the answer. The first one has been done for you.

What did the adoring squirrel say to his date?

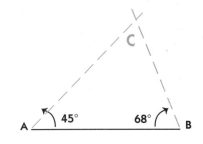

□∠ C = **67°**
REALLY

□∠ F = _____
I'M

D _____ 90° ____ 48° ___ E

□∠ I = _____
YOU,

□∠ L = _____
ABOUT

35° K
84°
J

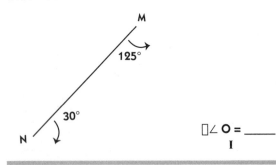

M
125°
30°
N

□∠ O = _____
I

P _ 60° ____ 60° _ Q

□∠ R = _____
JUST

S
74°
63°
T

□∠ U = _____
AM

□∠ U = _____
AM

V
60°
45°
W

□∠ X = _____
NUTS

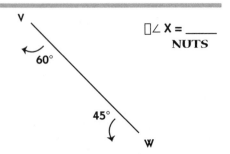

							really	
42°	60°	75°	61°	30°	25°	67°	43°

Name _____ Date _____

Rectangular, Circular, or ...

In this activity, you are given a line segment **S O** which is 1½ inches long. Complete the following seven steps using a protractor to solve the riddle.

For comfort, what shape did the octopi want their new beds to be?

1. At point **O** construct an angle of 135°. With a ruler or a straightedge draw a line from point **O** to make an obtuse angle. Measure 1½ inches from **O** and name that new point **T**.

2. At point **T** construct an angle of 135°. Draw a line from point **T** to make an obtuse angle. Measure 1½ inches from point **T** and name that new point **C**.

3. At point **C** construct an angle of 135°. Draw a line from point **C** to make an obtuse angle. Measure 1½ inches from point **C** and name that new point **N**.

4. At point **N** construct an angle of 135°. Draw a line from point **N** to make an obtuse angle. Measure 1½ inches from point **N** and name that new point **O**.

5. At point **O** construct an angle of 135°. Draw a line from point **O** to make an obtuse angle. Measure 1½ inches from point **O** and name that new point **G**.

6. At point **G** construct an angle of 135°. Draw a line from point **G** to make an obtuse angle. Measure 1½ inches from point **G** and name that new point **A**.

7. At point **A** construct an angle of 135°. Draw a line from point **A** to make an obtuse angle. Measure 1½ inches from point **A**. Your line should connect to the letter **S**.

O

1½ in

S

Unscramble the eight letters that were assigned to the shape you just constructed. Write them in the spaces below.

Name _____   Date _____

Hidden Question and Answer

Read the ordered pairs listed in the code boxes below. On the grid, find the letter of the alphabet that names each point. Label the ordered pairs on the grid with their coordinates to keep track of your answers. Write the correct letter in the box above the ordered pair. If the ordered pair appears in more than one code box, fill in each one with the same letter. Reveal a hidden question and answer.

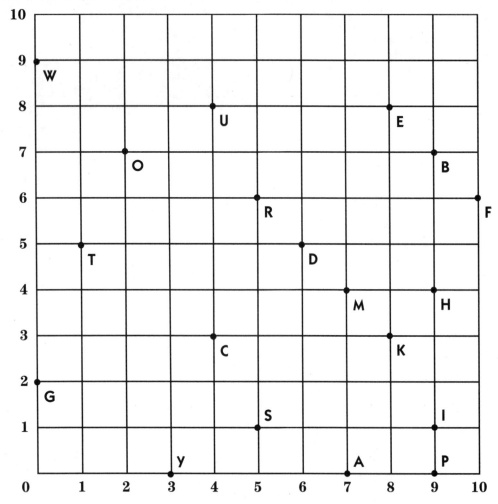

Question

(0, 9)	(9, 4)	(3, 0)

(6, 5)	(9, 1)	(6, 5)

(1, 5)	(9, 4)	(8, 8)

(9, 0)	(9, 1)	(8, 8)	(4, 3)	(8, 8)

(2, 7)	(10, 6)

(0, 2)	(4, 8)	(7, 4)

(4, 3)	(5, 6)	(2, 7)	(5, 1)	(5, 1)

(1, 5)	(9, 4)	(8, 8)

(5, 6)	(2, 7)	(7, 0)	(6, 5)	?

Answer

(9, 1)	(1, 5)

(0, 9)	(7, 0)	(5, 1)

(5, 1)	(1, 5)	(4, 8)	(4, 3)	(8, 3)

(1, 5)	(2, 7)

(1, 5)	(9, 4)	(8, 8)

(9, 7)	(2, 7)	(3, 0) |'

(5, 1)

(5, 1)	(9, 4)	(2, 7)	(8, 8)	.

Name _____ Date _____

Reveal a Hidden Shape

Read the ordered pairs listed below. For each ordered pair, mark a point and write the letter from the question on the grid. Join the dots in order with a straight line. When you have connected all the dots, a shape will be revealed.

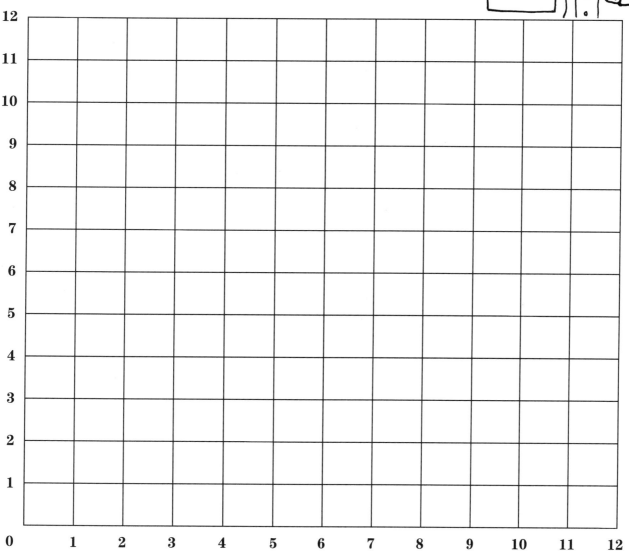

1. Connect these ordered pairs: A (4, 3); B (3, 0); C (6, 2); D (9, 0). **STOP** Lift pencil.

2. Connect these ordered pairs: E (11, 8); F (9, 5); G (11, 2). **STOP** Lift pencil.

3. Connect these ordered pairs: H (6, 8); I (3, 10); J (4, 7); K (1, 8); L (3, 5); M (1, 2); A (4, 3). **STOP** Lift pencil.

4. Connect these ordered pairs: H (6, 8); N (9, 10); O (8, 7); E (11, 8). **STOP** Lift pencil.

5. Connect these ordered pairs: D (9, 0); P (8, 3); G (11, 2). **STOP** Lift pencil.

Name _____ Date _____

I'm Hungry

Read the ordered pairs listed below. Make a dot for each ordered pair on the grid. Join the dots in order with a straight line. When you have connected all the dots, you will reveal the answer to the following riddle.

What food do snowmen enjoy the most?

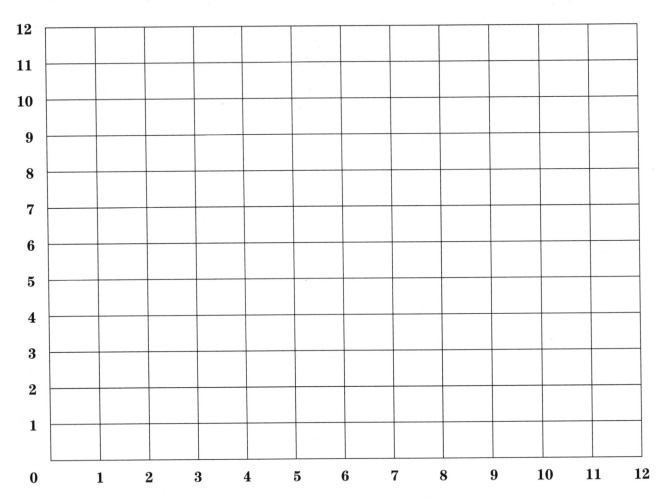

1. Connect these ordered pairs: (3, 8); (5, 8); (5, 6); (3, 6); (3, 8) (STOP) Lift pencil.

2. Connect these ordered pairs: (11, 8); (9, 8); (9, 6); (11, 6); (11, 10) (STOP) Lift pencil.

3. Connect these ordered pairs: (2, 6); (0, 6); (0, 10); (2, 10) (STOP) Lift pencil.

4. Connect these ordered pairs: (6, 10); (6, 6); (8, 6) (STOP) Lift pencil.

5. Connect these ordered pairs: (12, 2); (10, 2); (10, 1); (12, 1); (12, 0); (10, 0) (STOP) Lift pencil.

6. Connect these ordered pairs: (6, 2); (6, 0); (4, 0); (4, 2) (STOP) Lift pencil.

7. Connect these ordered pairs: (8, 4); (8, 2); (7, 2); (9, 2); (8, 2); (8, 0) (STOP) Lift pencil.

8. Connect these ordered pairs: (3, 4); (1, 4); (1, 0); (3, 0) (STOP) Lift pencil.

Name _____ Date _____

Fun With Line Designs #1

Complete the three line designs that have been started for you below. In the **right** angle, each ray of the angle is measured off in ten equal measurements. To create a line design, use a ruler or a straightedge and connect the point closest to the vertex on one ray to the point farthest from the vertex on the other ray. Now connect the second point from the vertex to the second farthest point on the other ray. Continue to connect all the points on opposite rays following this pattern.

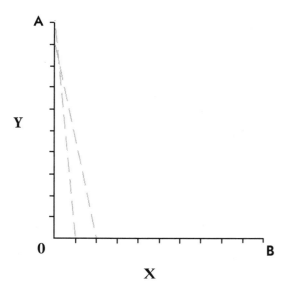

Now connect the points in the **acute** angle just as you did in the right angle.

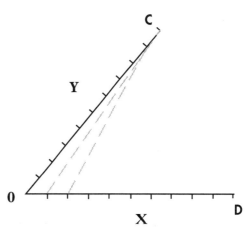

Do the same with the **obtuse** angle.

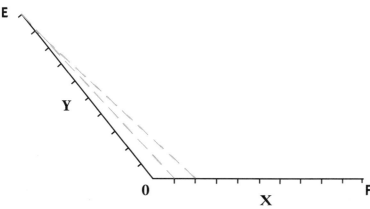

What do you notice about connecting points on rays that form angles of different sizes? _____

_____

Name _____ Date _____

Fun With Line Designs #2

In the shape below, two perpendicular lines create four right angles. Begin at ∠ **AOD** and connect the points as you did in Fun With Line Designs #1. When you complete the line design for ∠ **AOD**, proceed to ∠ **DOC**, ∠ **AOB**, and ∠ **BOC** and do the same thing. The four finished angles will create a complete design.

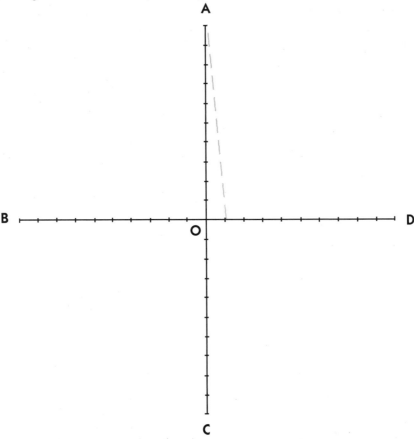

In the shape below, two intersecting lines create two acute angles and two obtuse angles. Begin with the acute angle, ∠ **LKN**, and connect the points. Then connect the points in the angles ∠ **JKM**, ∠ **JKL**, and ∠ **MKN**. The four finished angles will create a complete design.

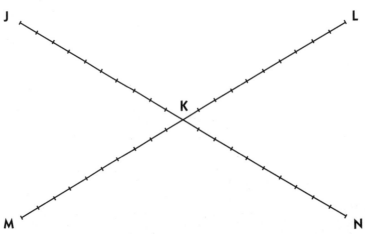

Name _____ Date _____

Fun With Line Designs #3

The shape below is made up of two perpendicular lines that create four right angles. The right angles are bisected to create acute angles measuring 45°. Each ray is divided into the same number of points. Begin with ∠ **AOB** and connect the points to create a line design. Move on to the next acute angle, ∠ **BOC**, then ∠ **COD** and so on until the line design is complete.

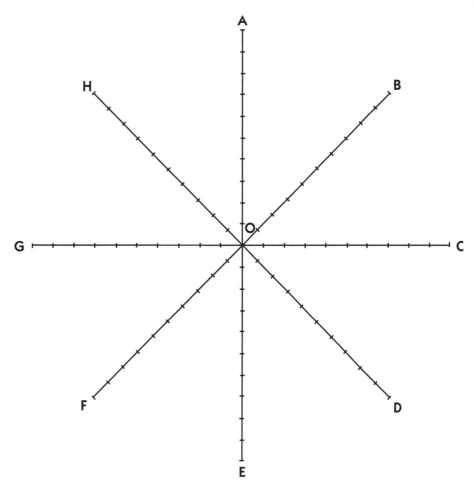

VARIATION A:
Create a shape similar to the above.
Connect the points of the right angles: ∠ **AOC**; ∠ **COE**; ∠ **EOG**; ∠ **GOA**.
Now connect these right angles: ∠ **BOD**; ∠ **DOF**; ∠ **FOH**; ∠ **HOB**.

VARIATION B:
Create a shape similar to the above.
Connect the points of the obtuse angles: ∠ **AOD**; ∠ **AOF**
                                             ∠ **BOE**; ∠ **BOG**
                                             ∠ **COF**; ∠ **COH**
                                             ∠ **DOG**; ∠ **EOH**

Name _____ Date _____

Ski Vacation

Find the area of each rectangle below. Next, record the areas, from least to greatest, in the code boxes. Then write the word in the code boxes that corresponds with each answer. Complete all the problems to decode the following riddle.

When asked about his skiing vacation, what did one skier say?

STARTED
25
25

REAL
68
16

DOWNHILL
65
47

WENT
53
53

HIGH
25
65

THERE
98
47

I
18
18

ON
56
12

BUT
72
23

FROM
67
48

A
16
45

EVERYTHING
86
22

Least

Greatest

Name _____ Date _____

The Novice Golfer

Determine the areas of the following right-angled triangles and locate each answer in the code boxes below. Write the word from each problem in the matching answer space to solve the riddle.

Why was the first-time golfer wearing two pairs of pants?

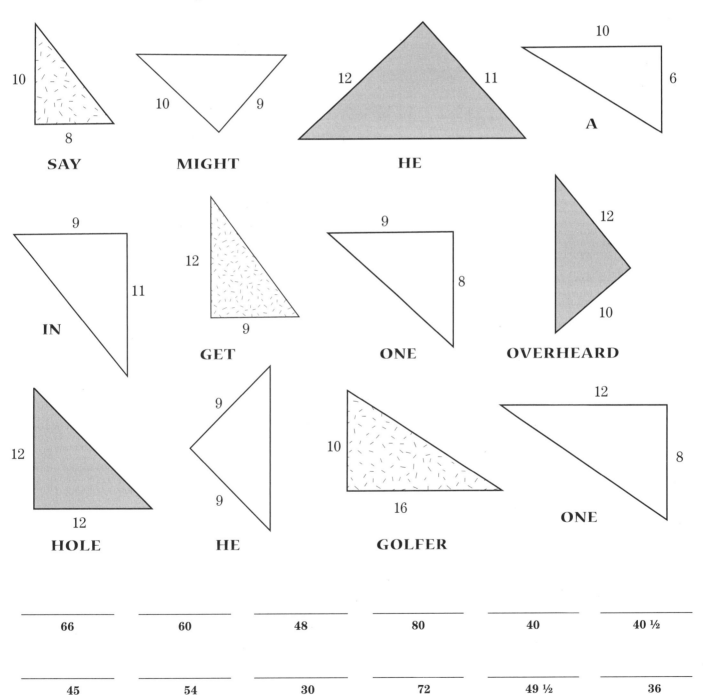

SAY   MIGHT   HE   A

IN   GET   ONE   OVERHEAD

HOLE   HE   GOLFER   ONE

66	60	48	80	40	40 ½

45	54	30	72	49 ½	36

Name _____ Date _____

Calendar Thief

Determine the perimeters of each of the shapes. Then, find your answers in the code boxes below. Write the letter from each problem in the code box with the matching answer to solve this riddle. If the answer appears in more than one code box, fill in each one with the same letter.

What happened to the petty thief who stole a calendar?

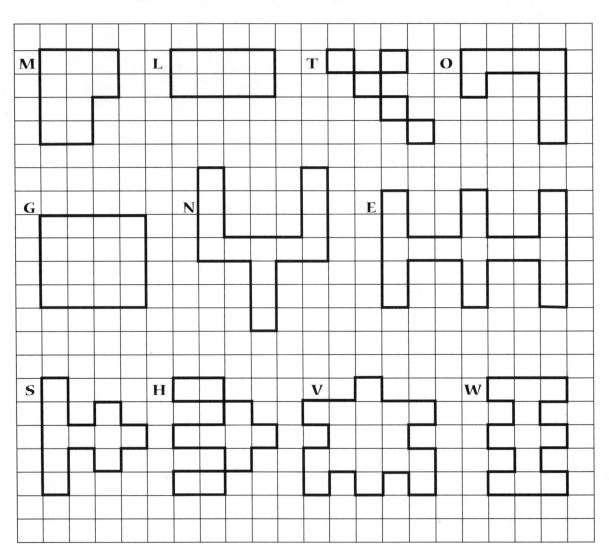

26	40

16	18	20

20	24	40	12	28	40

14	18	30	20	26	22

.

Name _____ Date _____

Sticky Stuff

Determine the perimeter of each of the triangles and quadrilaterals found in the figure below. Record your answer next to the problem. Write the word from each problem in the code box with the matching answer to solve the riddle.

What happened shortly after extra-sticky glue was invented?

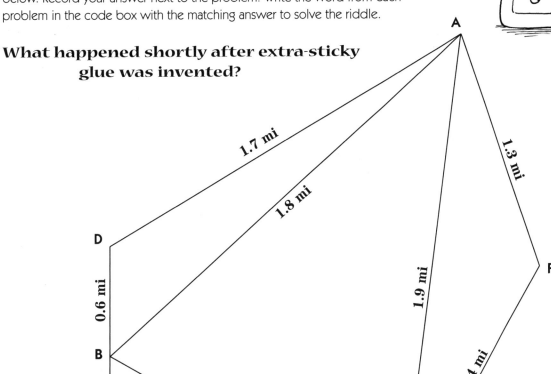

DBA	=		=	BECAME		DBCA	=		=	PEOPLE
BEC	=		=	IT		BECA	=		=	TO
ABC	=		=	ATTACHED		ABCF	=		=	VERY
ACF	=		=	OF		DECA	=		=	LOTS

6.2	4.6	5.8	4.1	6.1	5.3	5.7	3.6

SCHOLASTIC PROFESSIONAL BOOKS

Name _____ Date _____

Humpless Camel

Determine the volume of the following rectangular prisms. (The length, width, and height are provided.) Next, find your answers in the code boxes below. Then, write the letter from each problem in the code box with the matching answer. If the answer appears in more than one code box, fill in each one with the same letter.

What name was given to the baby camel that didn't have a hump?

L= 7, W= 6, H= 5 = _____ = D

L= 8, W= 4, H= 4 = _____ = N

L= 8, W= 7, H= 8 = _____ = U

L= 7, W= 5, H= 5 = _____ = O

L= 7, W= 7, H= 9 = _____ = I

L= 8, W= 5, H= 8 = _____ = P

L= 5, W= 5, H= 5 = _____ = E

L= 6, W= 5, H= 8 = _____ = S

L= 7, W= 5, H= 3 = _____ = M

L= 9, W= 9, H= 8 = _____ = H

L= 6, W= 6, H= 5 = _____ = F

L= 9, W= 6, H= 7 = _____ = L

L= 4, W= 3, H= 7 = _____ = A

L= 4, W= 3, H= 6 = _____ = T

L= 3, W= 3, H= 3 = _____ = R

L= 4, W= 3, H= 9 = _____ = Y

L= 5, W= 4, H= 7 = _____ = C

| 648 | 441 | 240 | | 320 | 84 | 27 | 125 | 128 | 72 | 240 |

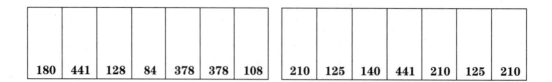

| 180 | 441 | 128 | 84 | 378 | 378 | 108 | | 210 | 125 | 140 | 441 | 210 | 125 | 210 |

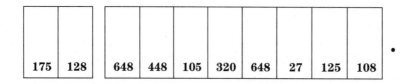

| 175 | 128 | | 648 | 448 | 105 | 320 | 648 | 27 | 125 | 108 |

•

SCHOLASTIC PROFESSIONAL BOOKS

Name _____ Date _____

The Coach's Advice

Find the volume of each figure. Then find your answer in the code boxes below. Write the word from each problem in the code box with the matching answer to solve the following riddle.

What did the coach say to his snowboarder at the beginning of the race?

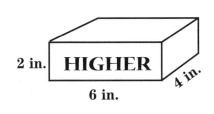

2 in. HIGHER 4 in. 6 in.

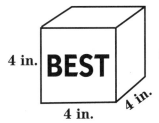

4 in. BEST 4 in. 4 in.

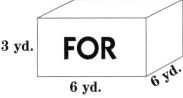

3 yd. FOR 6 yd. 6 yd.

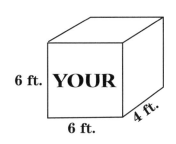

6 ft. YOUR 6 ft. 4 ft.

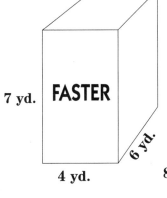

7 yd. FASTER 4 yd. 6 yd.

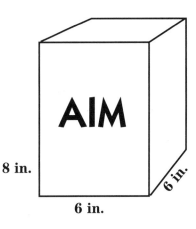

AIM 8 in. 6 in. 6 in.

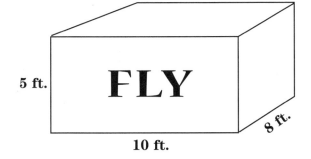

5 ft. FLY 10 ft. 8 ft.

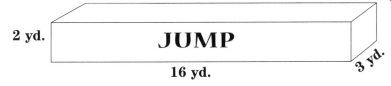

5 in. PERSONAL 8 in. 4 in.

2 yd. JUMP 16 yd. 3 yd.

									.
400	168	96	48	288	108	144	160	64	

Name _____ Date _____

Equal Values

Solve the problems below. Then match each answer to an equivalent answer in the code boxes. Discover the answer to the following riddle by writing each word in the code box that contains the matching answer. One example has been done for you.

What dietary changes did the doctor prescribe to the patient?

240 seconds = __4__ minutes
THE

72 hours = _____ days
SUGGESTED

$\frac{1}{2}$ hour = _____ minutes
THAT

13 min. 24 sec. = ____ sec.
PATIENT

6 P.M. to 9 P.M. = _____ min.
OCCASIONS

48 hours = _____ days
RAW

168 hours = _____ week
ON

Jan. + Apr. = _____ days
MEAT

1 hour = _____ minutes
DOCTOR

300 minutes = _____ hours
HIS

4 hrs. 38 min. = _____ min.
RARE

90 seconds = _____ minutes
EAT

THE			
4	60	3	30

5	804	$1\frac{1}{2}$	2

61	1	278	180

Name _____ Date _____

Links

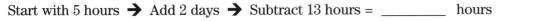

Solve each problem, working from left to right. When you finish a problem, locate the answer in the code box below, and write the word above the answer to solve the riddle.

Why was the lumberjack fired from his job?

Start with 5 hours ➜ Add 2 days ➜ Subtract 13 hours = _____ hours   = **AND**

Start with 5 days ➜ Subtract 4 hours ➜ Add 28 hours = _____ days   = **HACK**

Start with 13 hours ➜ Add 7 minutes ➜ Subtract 60 seconds = _____ minutes   = **AXE**

Start with 52 seconds ➜ Add 8 minutes ➜ Subtract $\frac{1}{2}$ minute = _____ seconds   = **COULDN'T**

Start with 8 weeks ➜ Add 48 hours ➜ Subtract 1 day = _____ days   = **WAS**

Start with the month of July ➜ Add 25 days ➜ Subtract 1 week = _____ days   = **IT**

Start with 5 hours ➜ Add 90 minutes ➜ Subtract 30 minutes = _____ minutes   = **HE**

Start with 1 year ➜ Subtract the month of June ➜ Add 15 days = _____ weeks   = **THE**

Start with 7 weeks ➜ Subtract 9 days ➜ Add 3 weeks = _____ days   = **SIMPLY**

Start with 48 hours ➜ Add 7 days ➜ Subtract 6 hours = _____ hours   = **GIVEN**

360	61	502	6	49

40	57	210	50	786

31

Name _____ Date _____

Let's Play Bingo

Solve the problems below and locate your answers in the bingo grid. Circle the answers you find in the grid. Any five answers in a line horizontally, vertically, or diagonally is a **BINGO**.

4 hours **AFTER** 7:05   =

2 hours **BEFORE** 4:20   =

2 hours 20 minutes **BEFORE** 4:00   =

3 hours 11 minutes **BEFORE** 10:00   =

4 hours 4 minutes **AFTER** 2:59   =

47 minutes **AFTER** 2:50   =

28 minutes **AFTER** 2:45   =

15 minutes **BEFORE** 11:10   =

2 hours 20 minutes **AFTER** 9:10   =

5 hours 3 minutes **AFTER** 1:58   =

3 hours 40 minutes **AFTER** 2:45   =

6 hours **BEFORE** 9:42   =

59 minutes **BEFORE** 4:30   =

4 hours **BEFORE** 12:15   =

3 hours 30 minutes **AFTER** 7:30   =

BINGO

1:40	4:59	6:25	8:15	2:20
4:09	3:31	11:15	6:49	10:37
11:05	9:22	8:48	10:55	11:00
2:47	7:01	1:11	3:37	3:42
5:05	3:13	11:30	7:03	6:52

Name _____ Date _____

Splish Splash

Complete the following problems to solve this riddle. Write the letter from each problem in the matching code box below. If the answer appears in more than one box, fill in each one with the same letter.

Why did the flock of sheep fall into the river?

If a clock says 8:20, what time will it say . . .

1. $\frac{1}{2}$ hour later? = = **I**

2. $1\frac{1}{4}$ hours later? = = **N**

3. $2\frac{3}{4}$ hours later? = = **Y**

How many hours and minutes are there from . . .

4. 6:35 to 10:20? = = **S**

5. 5:00 to 9:43? = = **W**

6. 2:20 to 10:15? = = **T**

7. 1:47 to 9:15? = = **R**

How many minutes and seconds are there from . . .

8. 6:10:12 to 6:15:48? = = **H**

9. 1:26:48 to 1:28:41? = = **U**

10. 9:51:13 to 9:58:27? = = **D**

11. 1:23:40 to 1:25:20? = = **E**

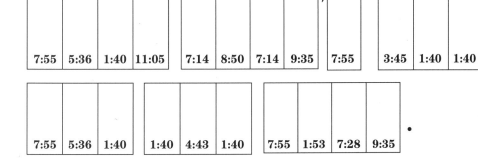

| 7:55 | 5:36 | 1:40 | 11:05 | | 7:14 | 8:50 | 7:14 | 9:35 | | 7:55 | | 3:45 | 1:40 | 1:40 |

| 7:55 | 5:36 | 1:40 | | 1:40 | 4:43 | 1:40 | | 7:55 | 1:53 | 7:28 | 9:35 |

33

Name _____ Date _____

Cinderella

Measure each of the following line segments in **centimeters.** Then find the total length for the open figure. Write your answer in the space provided. Write the word from each problem in the code box with the matching answer to solve the following riddle.

Why did the coach ask Cinderella to quit the baseball team?

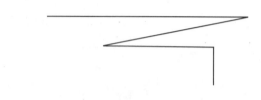

= _____ ALWAYS

= _____ FROM

= _____ THE

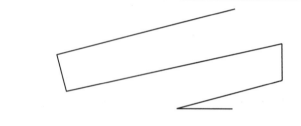

= _____ SHE

= _____ RUNNING

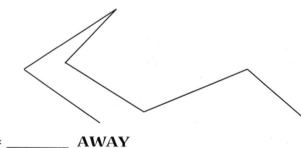

= _____ AWAY

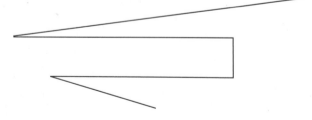

= _____ BALL

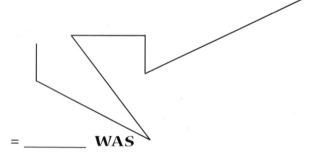

= _____ WAS

17.5	16	13.5	20	15	21.5	19.5	23	•

Name _____ Date _____

Sign on the Vet's Door

In the grid below, locate and circle fifteen three-number groupings that equal one meter. (The first one has been done for you.) All of the three-number groupings form right angles. When you have finished, 19 boxes will remain. Write the remaining letters in order from left to right and top to bottom to reveal the answer to the following riddle.

What did the sign on the door to the veterinarian's office say?

200 mm A	30 cm G	7 cm P	40 dm L	33 cm A	23 cm E	25 cm R	35 cm S
0.5 m L	16 cm A	20 mm G	0.15 m T	27 cm R	4 dm H	13 cm S	400 mm A
2 dm E	68 cm R	3 dm N	600 mm S	25 cm T	100 mm C	400 mm E	14 cm O
15 cm M	80 cm E	38 cm A	500 mm N	43 cm E	35 cm Y	4 dm T	20 cm O
100 mm S	1 dm T	300 mm I	12 cm G	0.15 m M	500 mm A	24 cm N	0.2 m E
30 mm S	7 cm I	0.25 m T	250 mm T	20 cm I	0.5 m N	2 dm G	0.6 m O
7 dm N	200 mm A	15 cm T	0.5 m D	7 dm F	300 mm K	29 cm W	61 cm K
15 cm S	10 cm Z	48 cm T	10 cm B	200 mm M	0.3 m A	1 dm C	0.5 m Y

____ ____ ____ ____ ____ , ____ ____ ____ ____ ____ ____ ,

____ ____ ____ , ____ ____ ____ ____ .

Name _____ Date _____

Match It #2

Match the measurements on the left side of the page to the equivalent measurements on the right. Use a ruler or straightedge to draw a line from one measurement to the equivalent (dot to dot). Your line will pass through a number and a letter. The number tells you where to write your letter on the lines below to answer the riddle.

What's a riddle book about eggs called?

3 ft 7 in •   • 1 ft 5 in

3,520 yd •   **7**   • 1 yd 5 in

                        L   **2**   **10**   **O**

17 in •   • 2 mi

39 in •   • 5 ft

                    A   **O**   **T**

1 mi •   **11**   **I**   **4**   • 1 in

60 in •   **8**   **1**   **12**   • 1 yd 7 in

2 ft 11 in •   • 1 yd 3 in

                    K   **5**

$\frac{1}{12}$ ft •   **Y**   • $\frac{1}{4}$ mi

2 ft 17 in •   **K**   **S**   • 35 in

                                          3

1 ft 16 in •   **6**   **B**   • $\frac{1}{2}$ ft

                                    9

6 in •   **O**   • 5,280 ft

440 yd •   • 2 ft 4 in

,

___ ___ ___ ___ ___ ___ ___ ___   ___ ___ ___ ___ .
 1   2   3   4   5   6   7   8   9 10 11 12

Name _____ Date _____

Tic-Tac-Toe

Complete all of the problems below. (Be sure to simplify your answer.) Look at
the digit that indicates the larger unit in each answer. If the digit is an even number, give that space an **X**, but if the digit is an odd number, give it an **O**. Any three
Xs or **O**s in a straight line wins.

6 ft 9 in + 3 ft 4 in	12 yd 2 ft + 7 yd 2 ft	10 ft 7 in + 8 ft 10 in
7 yd 2 ft + 5 yd 2 ft	5 ft 8 in + 6 ft 6 in	6 yd 2 ft + 3 yd 1 ft
8 ft 8 in + 4 ft 7 in	9 yd 1 ft + 9 yd 2 ft	7 ft 9 in + 9 ft 9 in

SCHOLASTIC PROFESSIONAL BOOKS FUN INDEPENDENT PRACTICE PAGES: GEOMETRY AND MEASUREMENT

Name _____   Date _____

Crack the Code

Calculate the totals for these units of liquid measurement and find your answers in the code spaces. Write the word from each problem in the matching answer space to solve the following riddle.

What did one teacher say about the boy genius?

IS 4 qt 3 pt + 3 qt 2 pt _____	**PHOTOGRAPHIC** 5 gal 2 qt + 6 gal 3 qt _____	**DEVELOPED** 3 gal 4 qt + 2 gal 3 qt _____
A 7 qt 2 pt + 6 qt 2 pt _____	**LAD** 3 cups 7 oz + 2 cups 3 oz _____	**NOT** 5 qt 4 cups + 2 qt 4 cups _____
THAT 4 cups 6 oz + 7 cups 6 oz _____	**THE** 8 gal 1 qt + 3 gal 3 qt _____	**MEMORY** 4 qt 3 cups + 3 qt 3 cups _____
AMAZING 8 qt 3 pt + 7 qt 3 pt _____	**HAS** 7 qt 4 cups + 6 qt 3 cups _____	**FULLY** 8 cups 5 oz + 3 cups 6 oz _____

_____	_____	_____	_____	_____	_____
12 gal	18 qt	6 cups 2 oz	14 qt 3 cups	15 qt	12 gal 1 qt

_____	_____	_____	_____	_____	_____ .
8 qt 2 cups	12 cups 4 oz	9 qt 1 pt	9 qt	12 cups 3 oz	6 gal 3 qt

Name _____ Date _____

Follow the Arrows

THIS WAY

THAT WAY

Begin at the ★. Solve the first problem and write your answer in the box directly below it. Follow the arrow to the next box and copy your answer from the first box. Solve the next problem, follow the arrow, and copy your new answer in the next open box. Continue to solve the problems, copying each answer into the next box indicated by the arrow. When you've finished the puzzle correctly, your final answer should be the exact number needed to solve the final problem. Go on to the second puzzle and follow the same steps you used to work your way through the first one!

★
```
  4 lb   2 oz
  6 lb  12 oz
+ 8 lb  12 oz
```

```
         − 7 lb 13 oz
```

```
  20 lb 7 oz
+  8 lb 4 oz
```

Express your measure of weight so you have the greatest number of the largest unit.

```
  12 lb 13 oz
+  5 lb 13 oz
```

```
  − 13 lb 2 oz
```

46 lb ←

★
```
  24 lb 13 oz
− 11 lb  2 oz
```

```
  7 lb 6 oz
  4 lb 7 oz
+ 11 lb 4 oz
```

```
  − 27 lb 15 oz
```

```
  8 lb   4 oz
  8 lb   3 oz
+ 7 lb  14 oz
```

```
  − 24 lb 15 oz
```

```
  14 lb 13 oz
   6 lb  8 oz
+  2 lb  2 oz
```

31 lb 10 oz

Express your measure of weight so you have the greatest number of the largest unit.

Name _____ Date _____

Office Closed

To solve the riddle at the bottom of the page, determine which of the three temperatures best answers each of the problems. Circle the correct answers, then write the words found under the answers, from left to right and top to bottom in the spaces at the bottom.

What might the temperature be if you were . . .

freezing outside?

42°F	28°F	36°F
HER	HIS	THEIR

taking a bath?

70°F	118°F	99°F
BUSINESS	OFFICE	PRACTICE

making a tray of ice cubes?

20°F	40°F	32°F
DECLINED	DROPPED	FAILED

swimming at the beach?

86°F	68°F	72°F
BECAUSE	SINCE	THEREFORE

experiencing a fever?

102°F	98°F	96°F
HE	THEY	SHE

boiling soup in a pot?

212°F	100°F	75°F
HAD	POSSESSED	HAS

relaxing in a warm room?

60°F	70°F	84°F
FEW	NO	MANY

playing outside on a hot summer day?

60°F	95°F	70°F
MANNERS	PATIENCE	PATIENTS

Why did the doctor go out of business?

_____ _____ _____ _____

_____ _____ _____ _____ .

Name _____ Date _____

Measuring Temperature

To solve this riddle, figure out the **Temperature Now** in the problems below. Record your answers in the space provided. Then locate your answer in the code below and write the letter from the problem in the matching code space. As you find identical answers, give those answers the same letter.

Why was the archaeologist down in the dumps?

Temperature Was		Temperature Dropped		Temperature Now		
6°C	→	12°C	→	_____	=	**R**
17°C	→	13°C	→	_____	=	**H**
-24°C	→	10°C	→	_____	=	**D**
15°C	→	15°C	→	_____	=	**I**
0°C	→	14°C	→	_____	=	**C**

Temperature Was		Temperature Rose		Temperature Now		
-26°C	→	18°C	→	_____	=	**E**
6°C	→	13°C	→	_____	=	**N**
-4°C	→	12°C	→	_____	=	**U**
13°C	→	8°C	→	_____	=	**S**
-24°C	→	26°C	→	_____	=	**A**

4°C	0°C	21°C

-14°C	2°C	-6°C	-8°C	-8°C	-6°C

-8°C	19°C	-34°C	-8°C	-34°C

0°C	19°C

-6°C	8°C	0°C	19°C	21°C

.

Name _____ Date _____

Word Problems #1

Write the answer to each problem in the space provided. Locate your answer in the boxes below, then write the word that is next to your answer in that box. Continue answering all the questions until you have decoded the following riddle.

Why was the gymnast such a special person?

1. Mr. Edwards leaves his house at 7:55 A.M. After traveling for one hour and twenty minutes, he arrives at his office. What time is it when he walks through the door of his office? _____ = FOR

2. Sydney completed his homework at 8:15. It had taken him 35 minutes to do his assignments. What time did he start? _____ = OVER

3. Mrs. Conrad's class went on a field trip to the zoo. The bus left the school at 10:05 and arrived at their destination three-quarters of an hour later. What time did the bus arrive at the zoo? _____ = SHE

4. Mr. Khan painted his wooden fence nonstop from 10:35 in the morning until 2:20 in the afternoon. How long was he painting? _____ = ALWAYS

5. At 1:45 an announcement was made that the cross-country race would begin in half an hour. When would the race start? _____ = BENDING

6. Jacqueline delivers newspapers on Monday through Saturday. She spends 280 minutes delivering papers. How many hours and minutes are spent on her paper route? _____ = PEOPLE

7. Jennifer ran around her block in 4 minutes 37 seconds. Julia ran the same distance in 4 minutes 56 seconds. How much faster was Jennifer? _____ = WAS

8. A thunderstorm started at 8:39 in the morning and ended at noon. How long was the storm? _____ = BACKWARD

10:50	19 sec	3 h 45 min	2:15

7:40	3 h 21 min	9:15	4 h 40 min

Name _____ Date _____

Word Problems #2

Write the answer to each problem in the space provided. Locate your answer in the boxes below, then write the word that is next to your answer in that box. Continue answering all the questions until you have decoded the following riddle.

What would happen if pigs could fly?

1. Ashley filled her aquarium using a measuring cup. Altogether she added 100 cups of water. How many quarts would that be?

_____ = UP

2. Three odd-shaped containers held 48 oz, 96 oz, and 32 oz respectively. How many cups would that equal?

_____ = OF

How many quarts and cups would that equal?

_____ = AND

3. The driver of a large dump truck filled his gas tank with 36 gallons of diesel fuel. How many quarts would that be?

_____ = GO

4. The Jones family was having a pool party for all the students in their daughter's class. Mr. Jones purchased 4 cases of assorted soft drinks with twenty-four 10-ounce cans in each case. Her classmates drank all the soft drinks. How many ounces were consumed?

_____ = THE

How many cups would that equal?

_____ = BACON

5. Hillsdale School placed an order with the local dairy for 660 pints of chocolate and white milk. How many quarts would 660 pints make?

_____ = WOULD

If the milk could be purchased in gallons, approximately how many would they need?

_____ = SIMPLY

6. A newborn baby girl was given 8 ounces of formula three times a day for a week. How many ounces were consumed that week?

_____ = PRICE

How many cups of formula would the mother need to prepare for one week?

_____ = UP

960 ounces	168 ounces	22 cups	120 cups	330 quarts

83 gallons	144 quarts	21 cups	5 quarts 2 cups	25 quarts

Name _____ Date _____

Word Problems #3

Write the answer to each problem in the space provided. Locate your answer in the boxes below, then write the word that is next to your answer in that box. Continue answering all the questions until you have decoded the following riddle.

Why do ghosts never lie?

1. A man with a voracious appetite went into an all-you-can-eat steak house and consumed 48 ounces of beef. Express this amount in pounds.   _____ = RIGHT

2. In a class project, a team of four students built a toothpick bridge. When the bridge was tested to see how much weight it could hold, it held 147 ounces before breaking. How many pounds and ounces did the bridge hold?   _____ = THEM

3. An elevator can carry 16 people or a total weight of approximately 2,500 pounds. Five people weighing 124 lbs, 163 lbs, 201 lbs, 89 lbs, and 53 lbs got on the elevator. How much more weight could the elevator carry and not go over its total weight?   _____ = SEE

4. A pick-up truck with a load of lumber weighs 4,400 lbs. The truck without the lumber weighs 2,400 lbs. How many tons of lumber did the truck carry?   _____ = CAN

5. A construction company was involved in building an office tower. A transport truck delivered steel girders to the construction site. Altogether there were 25 girders weighing 400 lbs each on the flatbed truck. How many tons of steel girders were delivered?   _____ = YOU

6. A caregiver provides snacks for the seven children in her care. Each child was given three one-ounce pieces of cheese. How many ounces remained from a two-pound brick of cheese?   _____ = THROUGH

5 tons	1 ton	1,870 pounds	3 pounds

11 ounces	9 pounds 3 ounces

.

Name _____ Date _____

Table of Measures

TIME

60 seconds = 1 minute	365 days = 1 year
60 minutes = 1 hour	366 days = 1 leap year
24 hours = 1 day	12 months = 1 year
7 days = 1 week	10 years = 1 decade
52 weeks = 1 year	100 years = 1 century
1,000 years = 1 millennium	

LENGTH

Standard	Metric
12 inches = 1 foot	10 millimeters = 1 centimeter
3 feet = 1 yard	10 centimeters = 1 decimeter
1,760 yards = 1 mile	10 decimeters = 1 meter
5,280 feet = 1 mile	100 centimeters = 1 meter
	1,000 meters = 1 kilometer

WEIGHT

Standard	Metric
16 ounces = 1 pound	1,000 grams = 1 kilogram
2,000 pounds = 1 ton	1,000 kilograms = 1 metric ton

LIQUID

Standard	Metric
8 fluid ounces = 1 cup	1,000 milliliters = 1 liter
2 cups = 1 pint	1,000 liters = 1 kiloliter
4 cups = 1 quart	
2 pints = 1 quart	
4 quarts = 1 gallon	

SCHOLASTIC PROFESSIONAL BOOKS   FUN INDEPENDENT PRACTICE PAGES: GEOMETRY AND MEASUREMENT

ANSWER KEY

Did You Hear? (p. 6)
1. Sides
2. Right
3. Semicircle
4. Protractor
5. Vertex
6. Congruent
7. Triangle
8. Rays
9. Compass
10. Acute
11. Circle
12. Rhombus
13. Obtuse
14. Angle
15. Degree

Did you hear about King Kong sitting on top of the Empire State Building?
Never mind . . . it's over your head.

Let's Talk Geometry (p. 7)
1. Angle
2. Protractor
3. Equilateral
4. Vertex
5. Triangle
6. Acute
7. Compass
8. Scalene
9. Right
10. Obtuse
11. Isosceles
12. Straight

What's the safest way to talk to a guard dog?
Make sure that you are as far away as you can be.

Match It # 1 (p. 8)

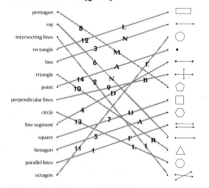

What should you do if Godzilla suddenly starts to cry?
Find an umbrella.

Look Out Below (p. 9)
W = 4, 16
E = 3, 8, 13, 14, 19
L = 23, 24
F = 21
S = 1, 12
R = 20
N = 6
A = 5, 15, 17, 22
O = 11
D = 9
H = 2

T = 7, 10, 18
Why did the little girl pour water over the balcony?
She wanted to see a waterfall.

Campfires Made Easy (p. 10)
7 = IS
3 = IF
8 = A
4 = THE
1 = IT'S
5 = ONE
2 = EASY
6 = STICK
9 = MATCH

How can a camper make a fire with just one stick?
It's easy if the one stick is a match.

Psst . . . Let Me Tell You (p. 11)
3 = STORY
1 = THE
5 = TOO
2 = TUNA'S
4 = SOUNDED
6 = FISHY

Why didn't the fisherman believe what the bluefin tuna was saying?
The tuna's story sounded too fishy.

Why Do Fowls Lay Eggs? (p. 12)
110 = EGGS
35 = THEM
66 = BREAK
15 = AND
45 = BECAUSE
41 = IF
55 = DROPPED
120 = THEY
30 = THEY'D
67 = DUCKS
49 = LAY
37 = HENS

Why do fowls lay eggs?
Ducks and hens lay eggs because they'd break if they dropped them.

Housebound (p. 13)
A = 55 = THE
F = 65 = TO
H = 75 = WAS
I = 75 = READY
K = 135 = HIM
M = 60 = BECAUSE
N = 60 = SNEAKY
O = 60 = ALWAYS
R = 25 = POUNCE
T = 40 = ON
V = 30 = CAT
Z = 20 = HARRY

Why was the little mouse afraid to leave his home?
Because Harry the sneaky cat was always ready to pounce on him.

Fly On the Wall (p. 14)
∠ F = 70°
∠ D = 120°
∠ D = 127°
∠ I = 65°
∠ H = 55°

∠ L = 135°
∠ G = 122°
∠ I = 50°
∠ C = 69°
∠ I = 71°
∠ C = 75°
∠ I = 40°
∠ I = 66°
∠ H = 60°

Why do flies walk across the ceilings in a house?
It's highly likely someone would step on them if they walked across the floor.

Why Are They Staring? (p. 15)
95° = 12
76° = 11
45° = 2
90° = 5
130° = 1
175° = 8
30° = 6
60° = 9
49° = 7
101° = 10
145° = 4
168° = 3

Why were the kids staring hard at the orange juice container?
On the label it said concentrate so that's what they were doing.

Squirrel Talk (p. 16)
∠ C = 67°
∠ I = 30°
∠ O = 25°
∠ U = 43°
∠ F = 42°
∠ L = 61°
∠ R = 60°
∠ X = 75°

What did the adoring squirrel say to his date?
I'm just nuts about you, I really am.

Rectangular, Circular, or . . . (p. 17)

For comfort, what shape did the octopi want their new beds to be?
Octagons

Hidden Question and Answer (p. 18)
W = (0, 9)
G = (0, 2)
T = (1, 5)
O = (2, 7)
Y = (3, 0)
U = (4, 8)
C = (4, 3)
R = (5, 6)
S = (5, 1)
D = (6, 5)
M = (7, 4)
A = (7, 0)
E = (8, 8)

K = (8, 3)
B = (9, 7)
H = (9, 4)
I = (9, 1)
P = (9, 0)
F = (10, 6)
Why did the piece of gum cross the road?
It was stuck to the boy's shoe.

Reveal a Hidden Shape (p. 19)

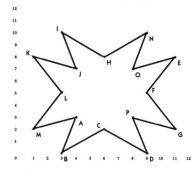

I'm Hungry (p. 20)

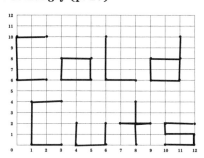

What food do snowmen enjoy the most?
Cold Cuts

Fun With Line Designs #1 (p. 21)

The lines in the finished design appear to be curved, but this effect is created by overlapping lines.

Fun With Line Designs #2 (p. 22)

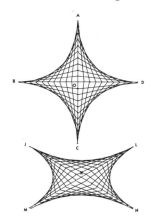

Fun With Line Designs #3 (p. 23)

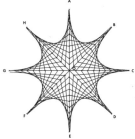

Ski Vacation (p. 24)
625 = STARTED
1,088 = REAL
3,055 = DOWNHILL
2,809 = WENT
1,625 = HIGH
4,606 = THERE
324 = I
672 = ON
1,656 = BUT
3,216 = FROM
720 = A
1,892 = EVERYTHING
When asked about his skiing vacation, what did one skier say?
I started on a real high but everything went downhill from there.

The Novice Golfer (p. 25)
40 = SAY
45 = MIGHT
66 = HE
30 = A
49 $\frac{1}{2}$ = IN
54 = GET
36 = ONE
60 = OVERHEARD
72 = HOLE
40 $\frac{1}{2}$ = HE
80 = GOLFER
48 = ONE
Why was the first-time golfer wearing two pairs of pants?
He overheard one golfer say he might get a hole in one.

Calendar Thief (p. 26)
M = 14
L = 12
T = 20
O = 18
G = 16
N = 30
E = 40
S = 22
H = 26
V = 28
W = 24
What happened to the petty thief who stole a calendar?
He got twelve months.

Sticky Stuff (p. 27)
DBA = 4.1
BEC = 3.6
ABC = 5.3
ACF = 4.6
DBCA = 5.8
BECA = 5.7
ABCF = 6.1

DECA = 6.2
What happened shortly after extra-sticky glue was invented?
Lots of people became very attached to it.

Humpless Camel (p. 28)
210 = D
125 = E
378 = L
128 = N
240 = S
84 = A
448 = U
105 = M
72 = T
175 = O
648 = H
27 = R
441 = I
180 = F
108 = Y
320 = P
140 = C
What name was given to the baby camel that didn't have a hump?
His parents finally decided on Humphrey.

The Coach's Advice (p. 29)
48 cu. in = HIGHER
64 cu. in. = BEST
108 cu. yd. = FOR
144 cu. ft. = YOUR
168 cu. yd. = FASTER
288 cu. in. = AIM
400 cu. ft. = FLY
160 cu. in. = PERSONAL
96 cu. yd. = JUMP
What did the coach say to his snowboarder at the beginning of the race?
Fly faster, jump higher, aim for your personal best.

Equal Values (p. 30)
4 min.
3 days
30 min.
804 sec.
180 min.
2 days
1 week
61 days
60 min.
5 hours
278 min.
1 $\frac{1}{2}$ min.

4 = THE
60 = DOCTOR
3 = SUGGESTED
30 = THAT
5 = HIS
804 = PATIENT
1 $\frac{1}{2}$ = EAT
2 = RAW
61 = MEAT
1 = ON
278 = RARE
180 = OCCASIONS
What dietary changes did the doctor prescribe to his patient?
The doctor suggested that the patient eat raw meat on rare occasions.

47

Links (p. 31)
40 = AND
6 = HACK
786 = AXE
502 = COULDN'T
57 = WAS
49 = IT
360 = HE
50 = THE
61 = SIMPLY
210 = GIVEN

Why was the lumberjack fired from his job?
He simply couldn't hack it and was given the axe.

Let's Play Bingo (p. 32)
11:05
11:30
2:20
7:01
1:40
6:25
6:49
3:42
7:03
3:31
3:37
8:15
3:13
11:00
10:55

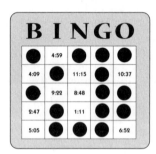

Splish Splash (p.33)
1. 8:50 = I
2. 9:35 = N
3. 11:05 = Y
4. 3:45 = S
5. 4:43 = W
6. 7:55 = T
7. 7:28 = R
8. 5:36 = H
9. 1:53 = U
10. 7:14 = D
11. 1:40 = E

Why did the flock of sheep fall into the river?
They didn't see the ewe turn.

Cinderella (p. 34)
13.5 cm = ALWAYS
21.5 cm = FROM
19.5 cm = THE
17.5 cm = SHE
20 cm = RUNNING
15 cm = AWAY
23 cm = BALL
16 cm = WAS

Why did the coach ask Cinderella to quit the baseball team?
She was always running away from the ball.

Sign On the Vet's Door (p. 35)

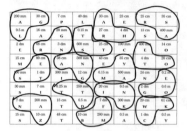

What did the sign on the door to the veterinarian's office say?
Please, come in, sit, stay.

Match It #2 (p. 36)

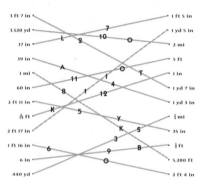

What's a riddle book about eggs called?
It's a yolk book.

Tic-Tac-Toe (p. 37)

X 6 ft 9 in + 3 ft 4 in 10 ft 1 in	X 12 yd 2 ft + 7 yd 2 ft 20 yd 1 ft	O 10 ft 7 in + 8 ft 10 in 19 ft 5 in
O 7 yd 2 ft + 5 yd 2 ft 13 yd 1 ft	X 5 ft 8 in + 6 ft 6 in 12 ft 2 in	X 6 yd 2 ft + 3 yd 1 ft 10 yd
O 8 ft 8 in + 4 ft 7 in 13 ft 3 in	O 9 yd 1 ft + 9 yd 2 ft 19 yd	O 7 ft 9 in + 9 ft 9 in 17 ft 6 in

Crack the Code (p. 38)
9 qt, 1 pt   12 gal, 1 qt   6 gal, 3 qt
15 qt   6 c, 2 oz   9 qt
12 c, 4 oz   12 gal   8 qt, 2 c
18 qt   14 qt, 3 c   12 c, 3 oz

What did one teacher say about the boy genius?
The amazing lad has a photographic memory that is not fully developed.

Follow the Arrows (p. 39)
★18 lb 26 oz → 11 lb 13 oz → 39 lb 24 oz
→ 26 lb 22 oz → 43 lb 48 oz = 46 lb
★13 lb 11 oz → 35 lb 28 oz → 8 lb 13 oz
→ 30 lb 36 oz → 6 lb 21 oz → 29 lb 42 oz = 31 lb 10 oz

Office Closed (p. 40)
28°F = HIS
99°F = PRACTICE
32°F = FAILED
86°F = BECAUSE
102°F = HE
212°F = HAD
70°F = NO
95°F = PATIENCE

Why did the doctor go out of business?
His practice failed because he had no patience.

Measuring Temperatures (p. 41)
-6°C = R
4°C = H
-34°C = D
0°C = I
-14°C = C
-8°C = E
19°C = N
8°C = U
21°C = S
2°C = A

Why was the archaeologist down in the dumps?
His career ended in ruins.

Word Problems #1 (p. 42)
9:15 = FOR
7:40 = OVER
10:50 = SHE
3 h 45 min = ALWAYS
2:15 = BENDING
4 h 40 min = PEOPLE
19 sec = WAS
3 h 21 min = BACKWARD

Why was the gymnast such a special person?
She was always bending over backward for people.

Word Problems #2 (p. 43)
25 quarts = UP
22 cups = OF
5 quarts 2 cups = AND
144 quarts = GO
960 ounces = THE
120 cups = BACON
330 quarts = WOULD
83 gallons = SIMPLY
168 ounces = PRICE
21 cups = UP

What would happen if pigs could fly?
The price of bacon would simply go up and up.

Word Problems #3 (p. 44)
3 pounds = RIGHT
9 pounds 3 ounces = THEM
1,870 pounds = SEE
1 ton = CAN
5 tons = YOU
11 ounces = THROUGH

Why do ghosts never lie?
You can see right through them.

Southwest Weaving: A Continuum

by Stefani Salkeld

This catalog is published on the occasion of the second
exhibition in the series *The Vision Persists: Native Folk Arts
of the West,* organized by the San Diego Museum of Man.
Southwest Weaving: A Continuum was on view at the San
Diego Museum of Man from April 1996 through February
1997.

This catalog was made possible through a grant from the
Lila Wallace-Reader's Digest Fund.

ISBN 0-937808-65-2

Catalog Author: Stefani Salkeld
Catalog Editor: Ken Hedges
Catalog Design: Les Roundstream and Debra Hart
Exhibition Curator: Stefani Salkeld
Color Plate Photography: Owen McGoldrick

Printing: Global Interprint
Printed in Hong Kong

Front cover
> Early Yei Rug; Navajo, 1900-1910
> probably woven by Yanabah Simpson

Back cover (diagram at right)
> a. Everyday Belts; Navajo, 1880s-1930s
> b. Everyday Belts; Hopi, 1960s-1970s
> c. Hair Ties; Pueblo, *circa* 1900
> d. Men's Dance Sashes; Hopi, 1890-1940s
> e. Wedding Sash or Rain Sash; Hopi, *circa* 1900

Previous page, top
> Hopi men spinning, carding, and knitting.
> *Circa* 1900
> From an Underwood and Underwood
> stereoscope card of 1908

Previous page, middle
> Woman spinning, with wool sack and
>   weaving implements around her.
> Navajo, *circa* 1940
> Photographer unidentified

Previous page, bottom
> Hispanic woman using homemade
>   spinning wheel (Northern New Mexico).
> Date unknown
> Photographer: Maria Chebot
> Courtesy of the Museum of New Mexico [9176]

*S*outhwest Weaving:

A Continuum is one of three

traveling exhibitions in the series

The Vision Persists: Native Folk Arts

of the West, organized by the

San Diego Museum of Man and

sponsored by the Lila Wallace-

Reader's Digest Fund.

Acknowledgements

John Hubbell, great grandson of Don Lorenzo Hubbell.
Navajo Reservation, Arizona; 1953
Photographer: Bill Measelle

The presentation of this watershed exhibit and its stunning catalog would never have been possible without thirty-four years of help and guidance by many wonderful people. They took me in hand, shared their priceless knowledge and experiences with me unstintingly, drove me onward with the gleams of insight and gems of learning that always made me yearn for more—and more. With them, I have worked hard, had great, great fun, satisfied endless depths of curiosity and the urge to know more, and have done my small bit to increase and enrich the already fabulous Southwest textiles collections of the San Diego Museum of Man. That, and this exhibit, have been my intensifying goals over the last three decades. My deepest thanks to all of you:

Ethel Porter Johnson, who so significantly helped build the collection and who taught me so much.

Jo Ben Wheat, great teacher and inspiration, generous sharer of the monumental knowledge he alone possesses.

Marian Rodee, good friend, always-willing teacher—warm, humorous, immensely knowledgeable.

Ann Hedlund, awesomely learned, writer of crystal clarity on just those subjects I most hungered to learn.

Martin Link, good friend for many years, endless source of first-hand knowledge which he always willingly shared.

Bruce Burnham, Reservation trader, deeply devoted to the People and their arts and their survival, another friend always ready to share and to help.

Robert Caparas, newer friend, equally knowledgeable and willing to share; entrusted with the responsibility of returning these priceless jewels to near-pristine beauty.

Ron Munn, dear, good friend of too many years to count, always ready to share his priceless wisdom and hard-won insights.

Irma Weimerskirch, immensely skilled practitioner of that art I find most daunting of all—re-weaving; without her talents and dedication, this exhibit would be, quite literally, full of holes!

Also, my heartfelt thanks to all the wonderful, willing helpers—interns, volunteers, and friends—who have lifted, carried, rolled and unrolled, staggered up and down steep ladders balancing heavy rugs, all the while having a wonderful time and (they said!) loving every minute of it: Ken Gary, Andrea Casillas-Hein, Laurette Zamora, Stacie Howard, and a host of others who have passed through the Museum's curatorial vaults over these many years. This never could have been accomplished without them!

Last, but in no way least of all, my inexpressible gratitude to the original creators of all these wonders, and to their ancestors, relatives, and the three endlessly engrossing cultures which are the source of their marvelous uniqueness and the beauty which they have created for so long—beauty which they have so willingly shared with the rest of us.

Stefani Salkeld
Curator, Southwest Ethnographic Collections
San Diego Museum of Man

Weaver with small daughter spinning. The child is possibly the once-famous "Elle of Ganado."
Navajo, 1906
Photographer: Karl Moon
Photograph from the Fred Harvey Collection

Introduction

From the collections of the San Diego Museum of Man comes this major exhibit of hand-woven textiles from the Pueblo, Navajo, and New Mexican Hispanic village cultures—three distinct groups who, at various times, learned from, stole from, fought with, teamed up with, and, overall, co-existed with each other.

They and their centuries of interaction have given our Southwest much of its uniqueness and fascination. This interplay is also richly evident in the textiles of these three peoples—so much so that many of us have believed that all Southwestern weavings have come from the looms of just one group—the Navajo.

One goal of this exhibit is to diminish the prevalence of that misjudgment; another—to increase awareness of and admiration for all of the remarkable people who produced these splendid textiles while engaged in a lifelong daily struggle to survive in an exceedingly difficult, often hostile environment. Whether creating essential elements of their survival—thick, warm blankets and winter wraps—or exquisite, symbolic expressions of the intricate, beautiful belief systems which nurtured and sustained them, these Pueblo, Navajo, and Hispanic weavers always strove to express their innate love of beauty, their respect for the bounty of Mother Earth and Father Sky.

The San Diego Museum of Man was founded in 1915 by one of the giants of early Southwest anthropology, Dr. Edgar Lee Hewett. Fresh from founding and directing the Museum of New Mexico and the School of American Archaeology (now the School of American Research) in Santa Fe, New Mexico, Dr. Hewett brought to San Diego his own personal fascination with and his vast knowledge of the American Southwest. He saw to it that the infant museum was richly stocked with hundreds of ethnographic and artistic specimens from this area he knew and loved so well. Over the past eight decades, the Museum's Southwest collections have steadily increased. Our close proximity to that region; the intense interest of hundreds of collectors, members, and donors; and the increasingly high profile of the Southwest Indian arts have all contributed to the enrichment of these collections.

Large, fragile textiles are difficult to exhibit in significant quantities and for long time periods—numerous problems of space, mounting, and other issues present themselves, always. The interest, involvement, and generosity of the Lila Wallace-Reader's Digest Fund have enabled us to meet these challenges and present our largest-ever exhibit of Southwest weavings—an exhibit truly representative of the breadth and depth of the Museum's extraordinary collection.

Southwest Weaving: A Continuum is the second of three exhibits in the series *The Vision Persists: Native Folk Arts of the West,* made possible by the Lila Wallace-Reader's Digest Fund. This trilogy, which also includes *And The Bead Goes On!* and *Fibers and Forms: Native American Basketry of the West,* showcases our extensive holdings of Western Native American folk arts. As part of the series, these rare collections are traveling to new audiences across the country for the first time.

For *Southwest Weaving,* the Museum's Curator of Southwest Ethnographic Collections, Stefani Salkeld, has put together a magnificent selection representing each of the three principal weaving cultures and covering their historic and contemporary weaving eras. To do this, she has drawn entirely from the collections of the Museum of Man. Creating this exhibit has been a source of deep joy, the realization of a long-held dream. Now our hope is that, in addition to fulfilling the goals set forth above, this exhibit and its catalog will assure a greatly widened awareness of the Museum's prized and priceless textile collections as a unique resource for researchers, scholars, artists, educators, and the descendants of those who created them.

Douglas Sharon, Ph.D.
Director, San Diego Museum of Man

Pueblo Textiles

Man weaving on a traditional Pueblo loom.
Hopi, 1879
Photographer: John K. Hillers
Courtesy of the National Archives

In the historical version put forth by non-Indian scholars, anthropologists, and technicians, the Pueblo people — descendants of the Anasazi — began to loom-weave around A.D. 800, probably using implements and techniques derived from Mexico and originating in the Andes even earlier, and the Navajo learned from them. Native peoples have their own coherent and satisfying explanations.

Pueblo textiles are, generally, far less known to us than those of the Navajo, but this was not always the case. When the invading Spaniards arrived in the 16th century they were continually amazed by the variety, quality, and sheer quantity of the beautiful cotton garments—often embroidered or painted—worn by the native inhabitants and given by them as gifts. Unfortunately for the Puebloans, the Spaniards' admiration soon turned to greed: one of the causes of the eventual Pueblo Rebellion against their Spanish masters was the sheer quantity of woven textiles demanded as never-ending tribute shipped to Mexico City, Madrid, and Rome.

Indigenous Pueblo dress consisted of breechcloths, kilts, belts, sashes, leggings or footless stockings, a variety of shoulder robes (often termed *mantas*), blankets, and rectangular one- and two-piece dresses. Formerly these were daily, year-round apparel; today most survive only for ritual use. The black manta-dress may still sometimes be seen at Hopi and the finger-woven everyday belts and hair ties are still frequently worn by Pueblo people. Among the Pueblos, except for a time at Zuni, men were the weavers and some Pueblo men, principally at Hopi and at San Felipe village in New Mexico, still weave, mainly for sale to other Indians. Thus, Pueblo weavings are seldom seen or owned by Anglos and much less is known or written about them.

Due to its age and to the focus of its founders, the Museum of Man has quite a number of Pueblo pieces in its collection, but—in deference to Native American feelings and requests—some will not be exhibited, nor will there be any commentary regarding their possible ceremonial usage. It is true that there are many such entries in the older literature and these are still available for study. However, museums today endeavor to be sensitive to native people's deeply-felt wish to decide for themselves how much, or how little, of their traditional beliefs and symbolism to expose to outsiders or to have interpreted by and for outsiders. We are extremely grateful to the Hopi Office of Cultural Affairs for its permission to exhibit several Hopi textiles and for their assistance with labels for these pieces.

Pueblo Textiles

Woman's Dress, or *Manta*; Hopi, late 1800s, *below*

Woman's Dress; Zuni, 1865-1875, *next page*

Married woman wearing manta dress,
two shawls, and commercial fabric underdress.
Hopi, 1904-1906
Photographer: Jo Mora

Detail of Woman's Dress; Zuni

Pueblo Textiles

Wearing Blanket, Pueblo or Navajo; 1850s-1870s (native repairs *circa* 1890), *below*

Wearing Blanket, probably Navajo in the Pueblo style; 1880s, *next page*

9

Navajo Textiles

Weaver with rug on loom.
Navajo, possibly Teec Nos Pos area; early 1900s
Photographer unidentified

The Navajos' own history of their weaving is told in the beautiful tale of Spider Grandmother, who taught Navajo women to weave on a loom constructed for her by Spider Grandfather—a loom made from red and white shell, Indian jet, lightning, streamers of rain, sun rays, all things most precious to the Navajo.

Classic Navajo clothing was very similar to that of the Pueblos — shoulder robes, rectangular panel or wrap-around dresses, semi-tailored shirts, breechcloths, and a variety of belts, sashes, hair ties, and garters. Spanish influence was evident in the use of wool — for in 1540, the Spanish brought the first sheep to the Americas and the Navajo took up herding. Their conversion from a formerly nomadic lifestyle to a pastoral one, begun by their partial adoption of Pueblo agriculture, was now complete. The Spanish also brought indigo dye, and *bayeta*—that rare red fabric dyed with cochineal (a cactus louse). Navajo women deftly unravelled, re-carded, and re-spun this prized fabric to use in their own weaving.

Spanish influence is also evident in those finest of all Navajo weavings, the wider-than-long, wrap-around blankets so closely derived from *sarapes*. But the clear similarity to the Pueblo styles of the times does not surprise us either, for we believe it was the Pueblos who taught the Navajo to weave while taking refuge with them from around 1680 to 1700, dreading the vengeful wrath of the returning Spaniards after the briefly successful Pueblo Rebellion of 1680.

Women's Wearing Blankets

Woman's Shawl, or *Manta*; Navajo, 1880s, *below top*

Woman's Wearing Blanket; Navajo, 1850-1870 (native repairs 1885-1895), *below bottom*

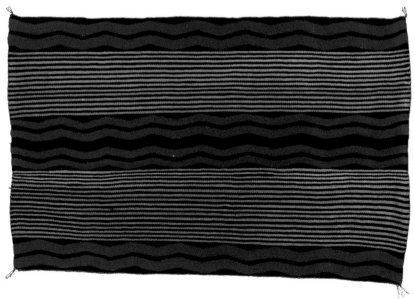

Spider webs are still rubbed onto the finger-tips of baby girls — for women are the weavers among the Navajo — to assure that they will grow up to be good weavers. So well has this been fulfilled, generation after generation for some 300 years, that Navajo textiles dominate both our awareness of and the market for South-western weavings.

To order our thinking about this enormous body of work we may classify Navajo weavings into three stylistic categories: Classic, *circa* 1650-1865; Transitional, *circa* 1865-1895; and the Rug Era, *circa* 1895 to the present. Superb examples of each period, from the Museum's collections, have been selected for this exhibit and catalog. Our only regret is that we could not include even more!

Before learning to weave — according to very scanty old accounts and their own origin legends — the Navajo wore clothing made from animal skins and various plant fibers such as strips of cedar bark. Regrettably, but inevitably, none survives today nor did so even into historic times. During the Classic era, Navajo weavers wove wearing apparel, principally for their own people but also, increasingly, for their Pueblo neighbors and other tribes with whom they had frequent contact. But their products were too fine and too gloriously beautiful to escape ever-widening notice — even traveling as far as the Northern Plains, where rare old photographs show Navajo blankets proudly worn by prosperous Sioux families.

Women's Dress Panels

Woman's Dress-half; Navajo, late 1800s, *below left*
Woman's Dress-half; Navajo, mid-1800s, *below right*

Woman spinning, with wool sack and weaving implements around her.
Navajo, circa 1940
Photographer unidentified

Classic Blankets

Man's Late Classic Wearing Blanket; Navajo, *circa* 1870, *below*

Wearing Blanket, a *Moki*; Navajo, 1875-1880, *right*

While the Navajos were imprisoned in eastern New Mexico by the U.S. Army, from 1864 to 1868, their own clothing gradually fell to pieces. Looms were few and sheep did not thrive on the barren, alkaline land, so the Army imported both Mexican sarapes and over 1,000 New Mexican Hispanic blankets for their desperate prisoners, and Navajo men and women were pressured to assume the post-Civil War clothing styles of the Army jailers and their wives. When, after four years of intense suffering and deprivation, the people were allowed to return to a portion of their homeland, these and many other changes were well under way among the surviving Navajo.

Within months, the first Anglo traders had set up business on the new reservation and the Anglo presence was everywhere: preachers and missionaries, government men and sometimes their wives, surveyors, geologists, and—within barely a decade—schoolteachers and railroad men. Their influences were felt in every aspect of Navajo life—including the weavings.

Chief Blankets

Second Phase Chief Blanket; Navajo, 1855-1865, *below top*

Third Phase Chief Blanket; Navajo, *circa* 1870, *below bottom*

Brulé Sioux Chief Spotted Tail with his wife and daughter, 1873
The women are wearing Navajo Chief blankets, a Second and possibly a Third Phase.
Photographer unidentified
Courtesy of the National Archives

Chief Blanket

Third Phase Chief Blanket; Navajo, *circa* 1880

Children's Blankets

Children's Late Classic Wearing Blankets; Navajo, 1870s

Transitional Weaving

Early Crystal Sarape-style Rug; Navajo, 1896-1903

Navajo weavers have always been keenly aware of the potential market outside their own culture and they have always been comfortable modifying their work in order to capture a sizeable share of this market. All this is manifest in the Transitional pieces—design elements from the much-admired sarapes of the despised Mexicans, partial border stripes (at the narrow ends only), and an exploding palette of colors as more and more red fabrics to unravel, and then aniline dyes, became available to them through the trading posts. These stimulated the weavers to concoct ever busier and more complex ways to include more and more of these vivid colors into a single textile.

This was the era of those incredible creations, the Eye-dazzlers—compositions of dozens and dozens of stair-stepped or zigzag, finer and finer lines, each of a different color. When the factory-spun and dyed yarns we call Germantown reached the traders' shelves, Eye-dazzlers reached their peak. Cotton twine as a substitute for the traditional wool warp thread eliminated the difficult, time-consuming task of warp-spinning, thus freeing the weaver to meet the tantalizing challenges to her creativity offered by these already-dyed yarns in a rainbow of dazzling hues.

Top: Reservation trader John Kirk with his sons, John and Tom, in their
Kirk Brothers Trading Post, near Gallup; 1930s
Personal snapshot; gift of Mr. Tom Kirk

Bottom: Kirk family members and Navajos in post wareroom; 1930s
Personal snapshot; gift of Mr. Tom Kirk

Transitional Weavings

Transitional Blanket, Early Pictorial; Navajo, 1880s, *below*

Transitional Blanket, Eye-dazzler with Hand-spun, Home-dyed Yarns; Navajo, *circa* 1890, *next page*

25

Eye-dazzlers

Transitional Blanket, Eye-dazzler with Commercially Spun and Dyed Germantown Yarns; Navajo, 1890s, *below*

Parade Saddle Covers; Navajo, 1880s-1905, *next page*

Eastern Reservation Rug

Rug with Both Ganado and Early Crystal Design Elements;
Navajo, *circa* 1900

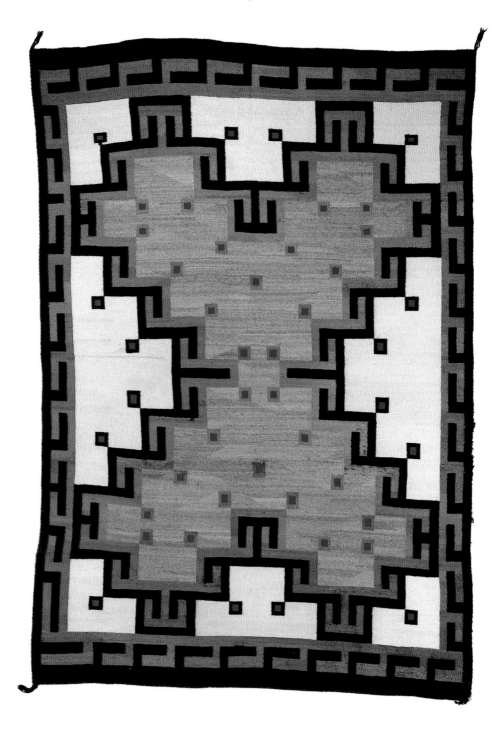

The market for large, room-sized Eye-dazzlers inevitably dwindled, as it did for the enormous rugs intended for the long *salas* and spacious rooms of wealthy Spanish and Anglo homes. But eagerness for the small, brilliant weavings known as Parade Saddle Covers has continued strong up to today.

In the 1890s, Anglo traders succeeded in introducing the Rug Era which, after several struggles to survive, flourishes today as perhaps never before. A great contemporary weaver's name will surely bring in a top sales price. "Name" weavers are stars at gallery shows, give lectures, teach classes—in short, are as lionized as are "name" jewelers, potters, and carvers. Their creations are eagerly sought by collectors and grace the collections of fortunate museums.

This was not always so: in the final two decades of the 19th century, most weavers strongly resisted the local traders' attempts to induce them to turn out what an Eastern or Midwestern Anglo lady could recognize as a proper rug—a bordered, rectangular, wool textile, its inner space plentifully filled with elaborate motifs suggestive of those found in carpets from the Orient, Persia, Turkey, and the Caucasus. The entire concept of a floor rug was foreign to the Navajo at that time—they had lived for centuries in their earth-floored hogans, sitting or sleeping, when they chose to, on sheep or goat pelts. Further, the enclosing of *anything* by a complete border was antithetical to them—everything made of living materials had a spirit that dwelt within it and this spirit should never be confined. One of the compromises the weavers first attempted was the single weft yarn continued from the central field out to the edge of a border. Some Anglo buyers were at first put off by this, believing it to be a mistake made by the weaver, so such a rug might not sell. Today, rugs containing spirit lines may be cherished by connoisseurs and buyers!

Ganado Rug

Ganado Rug; Navajo, *circa* 1900

Don Lorenzo Hubbell with weaver and her husband, bargaining
for a Moki blanket at Hubbell's Ganado Trading Post.
Navajo, 1890
Photographer: Ben Wittick

Two of the earliest traders to the Navajo were also the most influential in ushering in the Rug Era—Don Lorenzo Hubbell, at Ganado, and J. B. Moore, at Crystal Springs. Both these posts are on the eastern boundary of the vast Navajo Reservation and are not too far apart; thus, design elements, color favorites, and other such hallmarks of the early rugs frequently appear in the weavings from around both these posts. Yet each trader had his own favorite elements which enable us, today, to pinpoint the probable origin of almost any one of these rugs—the post near which the weaver lived.

Black (actually the natural dark brown of some sheep), white, gray, and plenty of red were the clear favorites of both Hubbell and Moore. Early in the Rug Era, when dyes were more difficult to obtain, weavers around both posts turned out many, many rugs entirely in shades of brown and tan—as did weavers all over the reservation during those years.

But when it came to design elements, important differences soon emerged, Hubbell repeatedly favoring a variety of crosses (none having anything to do with Christian religious symbols), Moore indulging his decided fancy for projecting "hooks" festooning nearly every solid figure in a weaving. Hubbell loved the old, classic, blanket styles and tried hard to save them in rug weights and sizes, but they completely failed to intrigue non-Indian buyers. Moore, meanwhile, supplied weavers around his post with examples of the Turkish and other carpets popular then in Anglo households, and Navajo rugs influenced by these sold well. Both Hubbell and Moore offered room and board during the summer months to adventurous Eastern artists in return for paintings of rugs which each trader felt sure would sell well. Many of these may still be seen around the wall of Hubbell's post at Ganado, now a National Monument.

Crystal Rugs

Early Crystal Rug; Navajo, *circa* 1900, *below left*

Early Storm Pattern Rug; Navajo, 1896-1911, *below right*

Early Crystal Rug; Navajo, *circa* 1900, *next page*

33

Klagetoh Rug

Klagetoh Rug; Navajo, 1930s

Klagetoh, a small, out-of-the-way post only a few miles south of Ganado, became known for rugs with a dominant center figure, usually called a "lozenge." This motif was often adopted by weavers around the two larger, better-known posts and spread from there to several other weaving areas, including Two Grey Hills, and to the pastel Burntwaters, which include identifiable elements from other posts as well.

While Juan Lorenzo Hubbell lived out a long and legendary life of more than fifty years as a trader — one whose name and fame are almost synonymous with the Navajo Reservation — J. B. Moore, who seems to have been almost as well-suited for and as skilled at the life of a reservation trader as Don Lorenzo, vanished forever from his Crystal Springs Post after only sixteen years there. During that short time, Moore and his wife, who also worked devotedly and hard with the weavers, had made an impact on the production of Navajo rugs still evident today. Weaving at Crystal Springs went into a three-decade decline following the Moores' departure, although a man named Molohon, manager under the Moores, remained there and did his best to maintain the former standards.

Two Grey Hills Rug

Early Crystal / Two Grey Hills Rug; Navajo, 1905-1911

Across the mountains, a small post named Two Grey Hills now began to emerge as a center for exceptional weavings. Two Anglo traders, George Bloomfield and Ed Davies, had come to this region in 1912 and worked together to improve and standardize the rug output here; previously, weaving around Two Grey Hills had ranged from appalling to indifferent. Weavers there had barely bothered to clean their wool, carding and spinning were haphazard, and little or no attention was paid to design, color schemes, and other rug aesthetics.

All this changed as with a thunderclap once Bloomfield took charge, and within a few years Two Grey Hills rugs were setting the standards of excellence for the entire Navajo Reservation. Indeed, in the 1950s and early 1960s, they were often termed "the Cadillacs of Navajo weaving"— an invidious comment no one, Anglo or Indian, would want to be caught making today! Two Grey Hills weavers decided to make their weavings known for the superb quality of their wool and each step in its care and preparation, the unbelievable fineness of their weaving, and their use of only the natural hues of the fleeces—just as they came from their own sheep. Absolutely no aniline dyes were allowed at first, but to achieve a flawless, dense, matte-black, a commercial black dye was gradually accepted. Later, some weavers introduced a very limited palette of a few local plant dyes, to enhance rather than alter the paler shades of their natural wools.

For a long time, it has been believed that the ladies of Tocito (a small post up the road a few miles), wanting to get in on the bonanza, imitated the output of Two Grey Hills, but upon being seriously threatened by those ladies, compromised by adding small touches of aniline red and turquoise to their rugs. And, indeed, there are some such rugs dating from around those years, the 1950s-1960s. A well-known authority on Southwestern textiles has, however, indicated his growing belief that this tale is apocryphal.

Two Grey Hills

Two Grey Hills Rug; Navajo, *circa* 1940

Weaver and family with loom and assorted belongings.
Navajo, 1897
Photographer: Adam Clark Vroman

Teec Nos Pos/Red Mesa Rugs

Teec Nos Pos/Red Mesa Rug; Navajo, 1903-1915, *below*

Red Mesa Rug with Simple Pictorial Elements; Navajo, *circa* 1900, *next page*

In 1905, a very brave young man named H.B. Noel opened a post in a wild and desolate region west of Shiprock where no Anglo had dared venture before. This was the domain of a resolutely independent band of Navajos led by the fierce Black Horse, who wanted nothing to do with traders. But Noel bought the finest rifle then available, practiced until he was a crack shot, and faced down a day-long intimidation by hundreds of armed and mounted Navajos who, at day's end, came to the conclusion that they (and their wives!) by now wanted that alluring variety of trade goods handily nearby. Noel hung his legendary rifle out of reach but highly visible behind his high counter, and the post he named *Tisnasbas*, or *Teec Nos Pos*, soon became famous for an ornately complex, vividly colorful rug with strong Oriental features possibly derived from Moore's favorites at Crystal, by way of Two Grey Hills. Here at Teec Nos Pos, and at nearby Red Mesa, the ladies added the widest, most intricate borders yet and accepted no limits to the numbers and varieties of brilliant colors with which they outlined one elaborate, zigzag line or complex figure after another.

Novelties

Wedge-weave (Pulled-warp) Blanket; Navajo, late 1880s, *below*

Illusion Rug; Navajo, *circa* 1936, *next page, top*

Pillow Cover; Navajo, *circa* 1900, *next page, center*

Tufted Rug; Navajo, 1965, *next page, bottom*
Weaver: Mary Louise Wilson; Kinlichee, Arizona

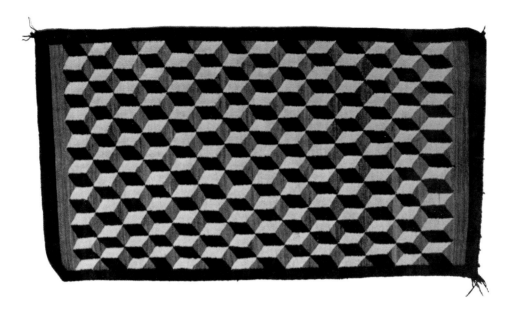

It was not only weavers living around a major trading post run by an innovative, deeply involved, Anglo trader who were trying to weave something that would sell to the increasing stream of non-Indian visitors to their reservation. Many tried various novelties: the pulled-warp textiles known as "wedge weaves," pictorials, mat-like rugs tufted with angora goat hair, small squares intended for use as covers for sofa pillows, two-faced and raised-outline rugs, and the so-called "illusion rugs" in which the pattern can be made to recede or come forward by the viewer's squinting or unfocusing his or her eyes while studying the piece. All of these sold, for short periods of time, to a relative few who came west seeking something odd or exotic as a souvenir of what was, then, an odd and exotic experience.

There were also weavings totally unrelated to the style of any recognized post or trader, yet still undeniably Navajo; these may be lumped under the term "general reservation" and are not much sought after. Then there are the infamous "Gallup Throws"—small, usually garish, having cotton twine warps and ugly, pseudo-Indian designs (often supposed Yei figures). These were named for the town where most of them were sold at the train station to uninformed travelers who had neither the time nor the willingness to spend money on something more worthwhile.

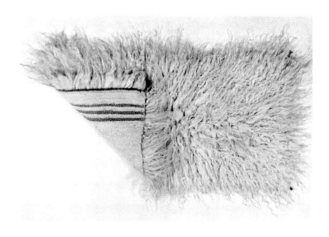

43

Pictorials

Reservation Scene Pictorial; Navajo, 1970s

Pictorial and the so-called "ceremonial" or sand-painting rugs have from the first been enormously popular with Anglo buyers. The first pictorials usually showed small likenesses of animals—often domestic, pregnant ones—and everyday implements such as feathers, bows, arrows, weaving tools, and alphabet letters used for their pleasing shapes, not as communication—at that time very few Navajos used or understood English. It must have been duly noted by a weaver, her family, and her neighbors that rugs containing such elements sold rapidly and for good prices, for their numbers and variety steadily increased. As more and more Anglo enterprises became important to the Navajo economy and lifestyle, business emblems, slogans, and other novelty designs were woven into rugs. These designs were later supplanted by American flags, houses, schools, airplanes, and vehicles, later still by detailed reservation scenes, Santa Clauses, and imaginative renderings of jungle landscapes containing wildlife of every sort, real or imaginary.

Unidentified weaver with pictorial rug, possibly at Gallup ceremonial.
Navajo, circa 1930
From an old postcard, photographer unidentified

The weavings showing likenesses of the Navajo Holy People, the *Yeis*, or delineating all or part of the dry-paintings used in healing ceremonies, caused much apprehension and resentment on the reservation when first woven for sale. The first single Yei is usually ascribed to the Navajo wife of the trader at Shiprock, who encouraged her and promptly sold the rug and as many as eight others she is believed to have subsequently woven. Many dire prophecies were made regarding her fate and that of her family and clan—indeed, the weaver herself did reportedly go blind in a few years. But, as financial gain followed this defiance of a strict taboo, other such rugs began to appear, woven by other women. Figures in such rugs are of the Yeis themselves, often stylized, or of the Yei-bi-chais—masked and costumed dancers who appear in nighttime ceremonies held on the reservation.

Weavers of sandpainting rugs usually leave out, or alter, certain significant elements well-known to them and to other Navajos but unknown to Anglo buyers. Thus the weavers hope to avert the troubles and misfortunes prophesied for those who render these powerful but ephemeral artworks in any permanent form, especially those obtainable by non-believers.

Pictorials

Pictorial Rugs; Navajo, 1880s to 1970s, *below*
Corn Yeis Pictorial; Navajo, 1930s-1940s , *next page*

Sandpainting Rug

Sandpainting Rug; Navajo, early 1930s

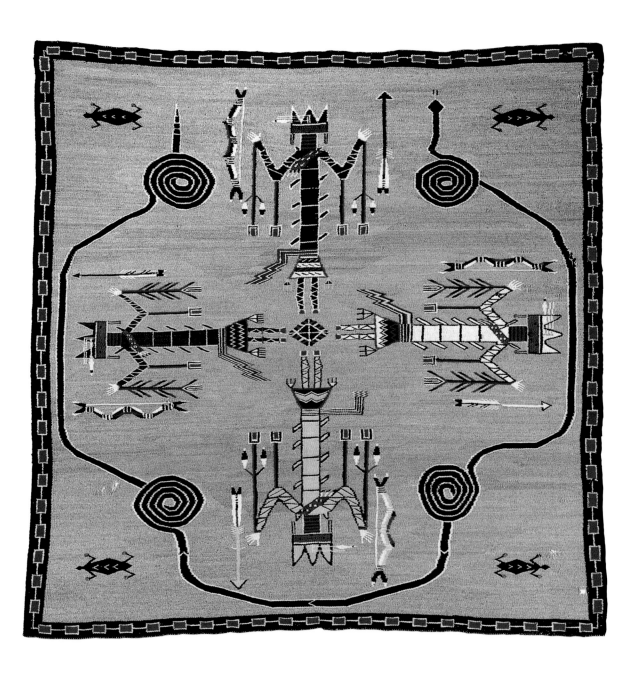

Yei-bi-chai Rug

Yei-bi-chai Processional; Navajo, 1942

Vegetal Dye Rug

Wide Ruins Weaving with Vegetal Dyes; Navajo, 1960s

Many more changes were under way, or still to come, as other traders and outsiders sought to influence Navajo weaving. At Chinle, at the mouth of Canyon de Chelly, one of the most revolutionary of all the changes took place beginning in the 1920s. This was the discontinuance of the bordered, red-black-white-gray, Oriental design styles and their replacement by borderless, banded weavings. These were dyed, first with lots of red and bright chrome-dyed colors, but in just a few years with soft, vegetal hues produced from local plants and minerals. The Chinle trader at this time, a man named Cozy McSparron, was apparently much influenced by a dynamic Boston bluestocking, Miss Mary Cabot Wheelwright, who deplored the old garish (to her) bordered rugs with their introduced, non-Navajo patterns. She urged a return to the simpler, Classic styles but in subdued, delicate tones and she even put up the funds to purchase every one of these from their weavers until the drastically changed styles caught on and sold well on their own. Another trader at Chinle, Camille Garcia, also claims to have instigated these changes, working with McSparron at around this same time; he feels that Miss Wheelwright had nothing to do with it.

From Chinle, this new, borderless, vegetal-dyed style spread rapidly to posts such as Wide Ruins—where a young, enthusiastic Anglo couple, Sallie and Bill Lippincott, did much to encourage it—and from Wide Ruins to nearby Pine Springs, where a soft, delicate shade of pink was favored. In the 1940s, borderless vegetal-dyed styles emerged at Crystal, where they supplanted Moore's styles and colors, at long last. Most recently, it has exploded in the intricate, pastel riots of Burntwater and Newlands. Both these styles were deliberately begun and fostered by local traders, most notably Bruce Burnham, around whose posts weaving was in serious decline, or where the nearby Navajo residents were being displaced. Lands the Navajo had long considered theirs were being returned to, or forcibly shared with, the Hopi, who had succeeded in reinstating their own claims to these same lands after long, futile struggles to do so.

51

Vegetal Dye Rugs

Chinle Weaving with Vegetal Dyes; Navajo, 1970s, *below top*

Chinle Rug with Vegetal and Synthetic Dyes; Navajo, 1930s, *below bottom*

Wide Ruins Weaving with Vegetal Dyes; Navajo, 1940s, *next page top left*

Crystal-Chinle Weaving; Navajo, 1970s, *next page bottom left*

Pine Springs Weaving with Vegetal Dyes; Navajo, 1960, *next page right*

Vegetal Dye Rug

Burntwater Weaving; Navajo, 1993
Weaver: Dah-bah Nelson, age 85

In the early 1970s, weavers at Burntwater developed the widest-ever range of pastel hues, using both natural vegetal materials—some, like Oregon blueberries, previously unknown on the Navajo Reservation—and a judicious selection of commercially-produced, pastel dyes to further broaden and enhance the weavers' palettes. These hitherto unseen tints, combined with the bold and intricate designs derived from areas such as Ganado and Two Grey Hills, have resulted in a stunning, unmistakable new rug which also has the economic good fortune to fit perfectly into contemporary "Santa Fe" or "Desert Southwest" decorating styles! In recent years, Burntwater has become wildly popular. Newlands weavers also use the pastel, vegetal palette but favor the design styles of the storm pattern, Teec Nos Pos, and raised-outline rugs.

Weaving is definitely alive and well on the Navajo reservation today. It is still principally a women's art but more and more men are allowing themselves to be known as weavers, no longer facing the stigma of being branded a homosexual, so feared in the past. The weavings themselves are changing, especially since the advent of the banded, vegetal-dyed styles—they have grown steadily smaller and finer and are now more wall art than floor coverings to be walked upon. There are a good many "name weavers" who enjoy national and international fame and whose name alone can bring viewers and serious collectors flocking to gallery shows. But almost all young Navajo girls have at least experimented with looms and yarns, so deeply is weaving embedded in Navajo cosmology as essential to the feminine ideal.

Young shepherdesses in Monument Valley.
Navajo, circa 1950
Photographer unidentified

Weaver Reyes Ortega at his handmade, European-style loom.
Chimayó, New Mexico; circa 1917
Photographer unidentified
Courtesy of the Museum of New Mexico [27978]

New Mexico
Hispanic Village Textiles

When the first Spanish peasant people were brought to the northern frontier of New Spain in the mid-1500s, the region had long been populated by the tribespeople we know as the Pueblos. Both cultures lived a very similar lifestyle — small villages based upon agriculture in a harsh land providing uncertain weather and growing conditions, little water, and exploitation by groups more mobile and more powerful than the villagers themselves.

Both were exceedingly devout, trusting in religion to aid them in their endless struggles to survive; both had a long-established tradition of textile production. One difference was that the Spanish herded sheep and goats—providers of wool—whereas, until Contact, the Pueblos had only native cotton and a few other plant fibers. Their many similar cultural traits enabled the two groups to coexist quite equably much of the time. Frequent raiding by the Navajo was also a strong unifying factor. Unfortunately, the Spanish government ignored the similar factors and concentrated upon religious persecution and unbearable taxation—thus bringing about the Pueblo Revolt of 1680. When the Spanish returned in 1692, they wisely moderated their earlier harsh controls and the two groups united, turning together—albeit unsuccessfully—against their common enemy, the ceaselessly marauding Navajo.

Meanwhile, village life had gone on. Intermarriage, frowned upon by priests of both cultures, inevitably occurred, and the results were evident in most aspects of life, certainly in the textiles produced. Wool largely replaced cotton, wool cards replaced teasels for carding, indigo was enthusiastically added to the native dye palette, stockings were knitted using needles instead of the aboriginal finger-looping.

Both cultures had traditionally woven blanket-like textiles as basic garments: the Pueblo manta was wider than long and was worn wrapped around the body horizontally; the Spanish sarape was longer than wide and might have a slit in its center so as to go over the wearer's head. Neither group abandoned its favored shape for the other, nor did they adopt each other's looms. But the Pueblos added bands of indigo-dyed blue to their conservative white-and-brown-banded blankets, while the Spanish apparently found that basic Pueblo pattern very pleasing, with the result that they wove it for themselves for the next several decades. Other such exchanges took place; European-dyed reds were sparingly introduced into some Pueblo weavings, as were a few other colors such as green and yellow. But Pueblo-Hispanic exchanges never approached the level of Navajo-Hispanic ones.

New Mexico Hispanic Weavings

Rio Grande Blankets; Northern New Mexico Hispanic,
mid- to late 1800s, *below and right*

The Navajo had been happily stealing weavings and weavers from both groups for more than a century and had more than a few of their own young people—principally women and girls—stolen in return. This hostile interaction resulted in more and more Hispanic and Pueblo elements showing up in Navajo weavings. A curious, difficult-to-detect class of textile appears in collections from the 19th century. These probably were woven by captive Navajo weavers who used their own upright looms but were significantly influenced by the choices—in colors and design elements—of their Hispanic village captors. Captive Navajo women, including the weavers, were called *criadas,* which translates as "servants" or "maids." For this reason, these blankets, formerly called "slave blankets," are now termed "servant blankets."

New Mexico Hispanic Weaving

Rio Grande Blanket; Northern New Mexico Hispanic,
1850s-1870s

Sheep grazing near El Santuario de Chimayó.
Chimayó, New Mexico; circa 1940
Photographer: Ferenz Fedor
Courtesy of the Museum of New Mexico [100373]

Of the many types of textiles once woven by the Hispanic village weavers of northern New Mexico, only two types are found in the collections of the Museum of Man: Rio Grande blankets and Chimayó weavings. I believe this to be because these two types have been most often mistaken for Navajo weavings. Rio Grande blankets, woven in the 1800s, were intended for use by Hispanics, Indians, and Anglos—all the folk then in the New Mexico Territory. They were made to wear, or for use as bed coverings—floor use wore them out too quickly, as some unaware Anglo buyers soon learned.

One especially vivid style, which blossomed in the late 1800s, was the Vallero Star blanket, named for its dominant motif—an eight-pointed star in multiple colors repeated in varying arrangements over the face of the textile. Its name comes from *valle*, the Spanish term for valley, for this design originated in the small, scattered villages set beside small streams throughout the Sangre de Cristo mountains north of Santa Fe.

New Mexico Hispanic Weaving

Vallero Star Blanket; Northern New Mexico Hispanic, 1890s

Street scene in Chimayó.
Chimayó, New Mexico; 1970
Photographer unidentified
Courtesy of the Museum of New Mexico [74184]

As Anglo influence became more and more dominant in New Mexico and the railroads brought more and more factory-made goods of every sort, these Rio Grande weavings were quite swiftly supplanted by commercial bed coverings, shawls, and other outer garments. The number of weavers declined sharply as Anglo tourists increased, all looking for something to take back home. A few of the weavers tried creating saleable — as opposed to the former, useable — textiles on their own looms. These comprise the second type most often mislabeled "Navajo" (or "Navajo?") in collections. This is the group correctly designated as "Chimayós." In many "Chimayós," garish colors replaced the old, soft dyes, and supposedly Indian designs such as the Northwest Coast thunderbird, or a version of the Mexican national symbol, might replace the classic, Saltillo-derived central diamond element. Not all Chimayó weavings were or are garish —

many still show the innate skills and artistry of their creators, most of whom are descendants of generations of weavers who still work on the looms of their own ancestors.

Although this centuries-old craft was threatened for a while, in recent years more and more New Mexicans of Hispanic and of mixed Hispanic/Indian ancestry have sought to learn from their elders, from surviving textiles, and from what records there are. We are most fortunate that these artisans and cultural preservationists are weaving beautiful pieces inspired by their own history and traditions. It is even becoming possible for some of them to earn a living and to gain some fame this way! As the collectors, museums, and general buying public gain knowledge and sophistication, we may hope to see this trend strengthen and grow.

Chimayó Weaving

Chimayó Blanket; Northern New Mexico Hispanic, 1930s

Hand-hewn Hispanic loom outside adobe house.
Northern New Mexico, circa 1935
Photographer: T. Harmon Parkhurst
Courtesy of the Museum of New Mexico [22681, detail]

Sheep flock and shepherd in front of Santo Tomás Mission church.
Las Trampas, New Mexico; date unknown
Photographer unidentified
Courtesy of the Museum of New Mexico [56328]

This exhibit then, is truly a continuum of the intricately intertwined traditions of Southwestern weavings created by the textile artists of the three great weaving cultures of that rich and fascinating area. Pueblo, Navajo, northern village Hispanic—each of the three could stand alone entirely on its own merits. No one of them does, although the Pueblo comes the closest. It was not encountered by the other two for thousands of years; then, within little more than one hundred years, it impacted and was impacted by the other two. Despite the violence and fury of these encounters, exchanging and sharing began almost immediately—sometimes forced but, more often, emerging from the totally human interest in anything new and different, therefore considered desirable and "pretty." Precisely these processes took place and resulted in the incredible array of weavings in this exhibit and its catalog. Now the members of the fourth cultural group to enter the mix, the Anglos, admire and desire the products of this amazing amalgam.

The San Diego Museum of Man, supported by the generosity of the Lila Wallace-Reader's Digest Fund, offers this exhibit and catalog with the hope that together they will add to your understanding of how such beauty came to be and simply enhance your enjoyment of it.

We-Wa, a Zuni man-woman, weaving on a waist-loom, or belt-loom.
Zuni Pueblo, New Mexico; 1879
Photographer: John K. Hillers
Courtesy of the National Archives

Bibliography

Amsden, Charles Avery
  1934
    Navaho Weaving: Its Technic and History.
    Santa Ana: The Fine Arts Press. (Reprint edition 1964,
    Rio Grande Press Inc., Chicago.)
  1988
    When Navajo Rugs Were Blankets. *The Indian Trader,*
    19(10): 6-8, 10.

Anonymous
  1974
    The Romance of Navajo Weaving. *New Mexico
    Magazine,* 52(1-2): 21-28.
  1976
    The Rug That's a Picture. *New Mexico Magazine,*
    54(2): 21.
  1976
    Long May it Wave. *New Mexico Magazine,* 54(2): 26.

Arthur Ross Gallery
  1994
    *A Burst of Brilliance: Germantown Pennsylvania and
    Navajo Weaving.* Philadelphia: University of
    Pennsylvania.

Baer, Joshua
  1986
    Collecting the Navajo Child's Blanket. Santa Fe:
    Morning Star Gallery.

Baizerman, Suzanne
  1989
    *Ramona Sakiestewa, Patterned Dreams: Textiles of the
    Southwest.* Santa Fe: Wheelwright Museum of the
    American Indian.

Batkin, Jonathan
  1986
    The Taylor Museum: A Tribute to Folk Culture.
    In: Josie DeFalla Kersetter, ed., *Colorado Springs Fine
    Arts Center: A History and Selections from the
    Permanent Collections,* pp. 43-126. Colorado Springs:
    Colorado Springs Fine Arts Center.

Bennett, Noël
  1973
    Genuine Navajo Rug—Are You Sure??? Window Rock:
    The Navajo Tribe and The Museum of Navajo
    Ceremonial Art.
  1979
    Genuine Navajo Rug...How to Tell. Palmer Lake:
    Indian Arts and Crafts Association and the
    Filter Press.
  1981a
    The Navajo Chief Blanket. *American Indian Art
    Magazine,* 7(1): 62-69.
  1981b
    Shared Horizons: Navajo Textiles. Santa Fe:
    Wheelwright Museum of the American Indian.

Blomberg, Nancy J.
  1988a
    *Navajo Textiles: The William Randolph Hearst
    Collection.* Tucson: University of Arizona Press.
  1988b
    Weaving a Legend. *Terra,* 26(5): 5-10.

Bloom, Lansing B.
  1927
    Early Weaving in New Mexico. *New Mexico Historical
    Review,* 2(3): 228-238.

Bourke, John G.
  1884
    Snake-Dance of the Moquis. New York: Scribner.
    (Reprint edition, 1984, University of Arizona
    Press, Tucson.)

Boyd, E.
  1974
    Popular Arts of Spanish New Mexico. Santa Fe:
    Museum of New Mexico Press.

Brako, Jeanne
  1993
    Recognizing Ethnographic Wear Patterns on
    Southwestern Textiles. *American Indian Art
    Magazine,* 18(3): 64-71.

Brako, Jeanne, and Bob Morgan
1988
The Care of Navajo Textiles in the Home. *Terra*, 26(5): 21-24.

Brody, J. J.
1976
Between Traditions: Navajo Weaving Toward the End of the Nineteenth Century. Iowa City: Stamats Publishing Co.

Brugge, David
1993
Hubbell Trading Post: National Historic Site. Tucson: Southwest Parks and Monuments Association.

Bulow, Ernie
1988
Navajo Weaving: A Critical Bibliography. *The Indian Trader*, 19(10): 14,18.

Burnham, Bruce
1985
The Traders' Influence on the Weaver. In: *Wool on a Small $cale*, pp.192-198. Proceedings of a seminar at Utah State University, June 23-26, 1985. Logan, Utah: Department of Animal, Dairy, and Veterinary Sciences, Utah State University.

Campbell, Tyrone D.
1986
Historic Navajo Weaving 1800-1900: Three Cultures —One Loom. Albuquerque: Avanyu Publishing Inc.
1989
Eyedazzlers: Navajo Weavings and Contemporary Counterparts. New York: Hirschl & Adler Folk.

Campbell, Tyrone, Joel Kopp, and Kate Kopp
1991
Navajo Pictorial Weaving 1880-1950: Folk Art Images of Native Americans. New York: Dutton Studio Books.

Cerny, Charlene
1975
Navajo Pictorial Weaving. Santa Fe: Museum of New Mexico Foundation.

Chapin, Harry
1988
Mae Jim—Master Weaver. *The Indian Trader,* 19(10): 4-5.

Colton, Mary-Russell F.
1938
The Arts and Crafts of the Hopi Indians: Their Historic Background, Processes and Methods of Manufacture and the Work of the Museum for the Maintenance of Hopi Art. *Museum Notes, Museum of Northern Arizona,* 11(1): 1-24.

Dedera, Don
1976
How Navajo Women Learned to Weave. *New Mexico Magazine,* 54(2): 8-15.

Dickey, Roland F.
1949
New Mexico Village Arts. Albuquerque: University of New Mexico Press.

Dutton, Bertha P.
1961
Navajo Weaving Today. Santa Fe: Museum of New Mexico Press.

Elmer, Wilma
1980
Navajo Rugs. Scottsdale: Carlos H. Elmer.

Elsas, Ellen F., and Ann Lane Hedlund
1987
"Well May They Be Made": Navajo Textiles From the Coleman Cooper Collection of the Birmingham Museum of Art with Selections from the Denver Art Museum and Private Collections. Birmingham, Alabama: Birmingham Museum of Art.

Fisher, Nora, and Joe Ben Wheat
1979
The Materials of Southwestern Weaving. In: Sarah Nestor, ed., *Spanish Textile Tradition of New Mexico and Colorado*, pp. 196-200. Santa Fe: Museum of New Mexico Press.

Fox, Nancy
1978
Pueblo Weaving and Textile Arts. Santa Fe: Museum of New Mexico Press.

Frid, Dianna
1994
Cochineal: Cactus Blood. *Fiberarts,* 20(4): 11-12.

Getzwiller, Steve
1984
Ray Manley's The Fine Art of Navajo Weaving. Tucson: Ray Manley Publications.

Goin, Chelsea Miller
1994
Design Origins: The Influence of Oriental Rugs on Navajo Weaving. *Fiberarts,* 20(4): 43-49.

Harmsen, W. D.
1977
Patterns and Sources of Navajo Weaving. Joe Ben Wheat, Exhibit Curator. Wheat Ridge, Colorado: Harmsen's Western Americana Collection.

Hedlund, Ann Lane
1986
Commercial Materials in Modern Navajo Rugs. *The Textile Museum Journal,* 25: 83-94.
1988a
Current Trends in Navajo Weaving: Art from the Navajo Loom. *Terra,* 26(5): 15-20.
1988b
Navajo Rug Designs Today. *Oriental Rug Review,* 9(1): 46-47.
1990
Beyond the Loom: Keys to Understanding Early Southwestern Weaving. Introduction and Observations by Joe Ben Wheat. Boulder: Johnson Publishing.
1994a
Contemporary Navajo Weaving: Thoughts that Count. *Plateau,* 65(1). Flagstaff: Museum of Northern Arizona Press.

1994b
Speaking For or About Others?: Evolving Ethnological Perspectives. *Museum Anthropology,* 18(3): 32-43.

Hedlund, Ann Lane, and Louise I. Stiver
1991
Wedge Weave Textiles of the Navajo. *American Indian Art Magazine,* 16(3): 54-65, 82.

Hillerman, Tony
1976
Going...Going... *New Mexico Magazine,* 54(2): 28.

Hollister, U. S.
1903
The Navajo and His Blanket. Denver: privately published. (Reprint edition 1972, Rio Grande Press Inc., Glorieta, New Mexico.)

Jacka, Jerry D.
1974
Hopi Weaving. *Arizona Highways,* 50(7): 2-4.

James, George Wharton
1914
Indian Blankets and Their Makers. Chicago: A. C. McClurg & Co.

James, H. L.
1988
Rugs and Post: The Story of Navajo Weaving and Indian Trading. West Chester, Pennsylvania: Schiffer Publishing Co.

Jeter, James, and P. Marie Juelke
1978
The Saltillo Serape: An Exhibition Originated by the Santa Barbara Museum of Art. Santa Barbara: New World Arts.

Kahlenberg, Mary Hunt, and Anthony Berlant
1972
The Navajo Blanket. Los Angeles: Praeger Publishers, Inc.

Kaufman, Alice, and Christopher Selser
 1985
  The Navajo Weaving Tradition: 1650 to the Present.
  New York: E. P. Dutton, Inc.

Kent, Kate Peck
 1961
  The Story of Navaho Weaving. Phoenix: The Heard
  Museum of Anthropology and Primitive Arts.
 1981
  Pueblo Weaving. *American Indian Art Magazine,*
  7(1): 32-45.
 1983a
  Pueblo Indian Textiles: A Living Tradition. Santa Fe:
  School of American Research Press.
 1983b
  Spanish, Navajo, or Pueblo?: A Guide to the
  Identification of Nineteenth-Century Southwestern
  Textiles. In: Marta Weigle, ed., *Hispanic Arts &
  Ethnohistory in the Southwest,* pp. 135-167. Santa Fe:
  Ancient City Press.
 1985
  Navajo Weaving: Three Centuries of Change.
  Santa Fe: School of American Research Press.
 1989
  The History of Southwestern Weaving. In: *I Am Here:
  Two Thousand Years of Southwest Indian Arts and
  Culture,* pp. 89-101. Santa Fe: Museum of New
  Mexico Press.

Lamb, Susan
 1992
  A Guide to Navajo Rugs. Tucson: Southwest Parks
  and Monuments Association.

Leafdale, Keith
 1974
  Weaving...Alive and Well. *Arizona Highways,*
  50(7): 29.

Link, Martin
 1988
  Navajo Rugs Styles and Patterns. *The Indian Trader,*
  19(10): 16-17.

Maxwell, Gilbert S.
 1963
  Navajo Rugs: Past, Present and Future.
  Palm Desert: Best-West Publications.

McCoy, Ron
 1986
  Navajo Child's Blankets. *Southwest Profile,*
  9(5): 14-17.

McGreevy, Susan
 1981
  Navajo Sandpainting Textiles at the Wheelwright
  Museum. *American Indian Art Magazine,* 16(3): 54-61.

McIntyre, Kellen Kee, and Eric Lane
 1992
  Hispanic Traditions Interwoven in Río Grande
  Blankets. *New Mexico Magazine,* 70(2): 50-57.

McNitt, Frank
 1962
  The Indian Traders. Norman: University of
  Oklahoma Press.

McPherson, Robert S.
 1992
  Naalyéhé Bá Hooghan—"House of Merchandise":
  The Navajo Trading Post as an Institution of Cultural
  Change, 1900 to 1930. *American Indian Culture and
  Research Journal,* 16(1): 23-43.

Mera, H. P.
 1943
  Pueblo Indian Embroidery. *Memoirs of the Laboratory
  of Anthropology,* Volume 4. Santa Fe: Laboratory of
  Anthropology.
 1947
  Navajo Textile Arts. Santa Fe: Laboratory of
  Anthropology.
 1987
  *Spanish American Blanketry: Its Relationship to
  Aboriginal Weaving in the Southwest.* Introduction by
  Kate Peck Kent. Foreword by E. Boyd. Santa Fe:
  School of American Research Press.

Mera, H. P., and Joe Ben Wheat
  1978
    The Alfred I. Barton Collection of Southwestern Textiles. Miami: The Lowe Art Museum, University of Miami.

Moore, J. B.
  1987
    The Catalogs of Fine Navajo Blankets, Rugs, Ceremonial Baskets, Silverware, Jewelry & Curios. Albuquerque: Avanyu Publishing Inc. (Originally published between 1903 and 1911 at Crystal Trading Post.)

Museum of Northern Arizona
  1981
    Tension and Harmony: the Navajo Rug. *Plateau,* 52(4). Flagstaff: Museum of Northern Arizona.
  1986
    Historic Trading Posts. *Plateau,* 57(3). Flagstaff: Museum of Northern Arizona.

Nequatewa, Edmund
  1933
    Hopi Courtship and Marriage. *Museum Notes, Museum of Northern Arizona,* 5(9): 41-56.

Nestor, Sarah
  1978
    The Native Market of the Spanish New Mexican Craftsmen: Santa Fe, 1933-1940. Santa Fe: The Colonial New Mexico Historical Foundation.

O'Connor, Patricia J.
  1992
    Warm Regards. *Spirit,* 50-55 (February 1992): 35-39.

O'Kane, Walter Collins
  1950
    Sun in the Sky. Norman: University of Oklahoma Press.

Ortiz, Alfonso, ed.
  1979
    Southwest. Handbook of North American Indians, 9. Washington: Smithsonian Institution.
  1983
    Southwest. Handbook of North American Indians, 10. Washington: Smithsonian Institution.

Reichard, Gladys A.
  1934
    Spider Woman: A Story of Navajo Weavers and Chanters. New York: The MacMillan Company. (Reprint edition, 1968, Rio Grande Press Inc., Glorieta, New Mexico.)
  1936a
    Color in Navajo Weaving. *Arizona Historical Review,* 7(2): 19-29.
  1936b
    Navajo Shepherd and Weaver. New York: J. J. Augustin Publisher. (Reprint edition, 1968, Rio Grande Press Inc., Glorieta, New Mexico.)

Rodee, Marian
  1977
    Southwestern Weaving. Albuquerque: University of New Mexico Press.
  1978
    Multiple Pattern Germantown Rugs. *American Indian Art Magazine,* 3(3): 44-49.
  1981
    Old Navajo Rugs: Their Development From 1900 to 1940. Albuquerque: University of New Mexico Press.
  1987
    Weaving of the Southwest: From the Maxwell Museum of Anthropology, University of New Mexico. West Chester: Schiffer Publishing Ltd.
  1989
    Modern Eye Dazzlers: Weaving of the Alamo Navajo. *American Indian Art Magazine,* 14(3): 7, 61.
  1995
    One Hundred Years of Navajo Rugs. Albuquerque: University of New Mexico Press.

Roediger, Virginia More
1941
Ceremonial Costumes of the Pueblo Indians: Their Evolution, Fabrication, and Significance in the Prayer Drama. Berkeley: University of California Press.

Sayers, Robert
1981
Symbol and Meaning in Hopi Ritual Textile Design. *American Indian Art Magazine,* 7(1): 70-77.

Simmons, Katina, and Carol Stout
1976
East Meets West. *New Mexico Magazine,* 54(2): 16-20.

Sotheby's
1991
The Lorimer Collection of Southwestern Weavings. New York: Sotheby's.

Tanner, Clara Lee
1968
Southwest Indian Craft Arts. Tucson: University of Arizona Press.

Thompson, Laura, and Alice Joseph
1944
The Hopi Way. Chicago: University of Chicago Press.

Tilley, Martha
1967
Three Textile Traditions: Pueblo, Navaho and Rio Grande. Colorado Springs: The Taylor Museum of the Colorado Springs Fine Arts Center.

Underhill, Ruth
1944
Pueblo Crafts. Indian Handcrafts, 7. Education Division, United States Indian Service.
1946
Workaday Life of the Pueblos. Indian Life and Customs, 4. Education Division, United States Indian Service.
1956
The Navajos. Norman: University of Oklahoma.

Ware, John A.
1989
The Southwest: An Overview. In: *I Am Here: Two Thousand Years of Southwest Indian Arts and Culture,* pp. 1-9. Santa Fe: Museum of New Mexico Press.

Watkins, Frances E.
1945
The Navaho. *Southwest Museum Leaflets,* 16 (second edition).

Wheat, Joe Ben
1974
Three Centuries of Navajo Weaving. *Arizona Highways,* 50(7): 13, 22-23,34, 42, 45.
1976
The Navajo Chief Blanket. *American Indian Art Magazine,* 1(3): 44-53.
1984
The Gift of Spiderwoman: Southwestern Textiles— The Navajo Tradition. Philadelphia: University of Pennsylvania Museum.

Williams, Lester L.
1989
C. N. Cotton and His Navajo Blankets. Albuquerque: Avanyu Publishing Inc.

Wroth, William, ed.
1977
Hispanic Crafts of the Southwest. Colorado Springs: Colorado Springs Fine Arts Center.